FRANCIS THOMPSON is the author of over thirty books. These include short stories, poetry booklets and several books about the Highlands and Islands. Born and raised in Stornoway, he has a vast knowledge of the Highlands and of Gaelic History. His deeply held beliefs that Scotland has its own identifiable and viable culture has led him to not only write about his beloved land, but also to involve himself in Scottish politics and the struggle to achieve full recognition of the Gaelic Language. He has recently retired from full-time teaching and still lives in Stornoway.

By the same author:

The Crofting Years, eighth edition 1997 (Luath Press)
In Hebrides Seas, 1994
Hebrides in Old Picture Postcards, 1989
The Western Isles, 1988
Shell Guide to Northern Scotland, 1987
The National Mod, 1979
Portrait of the River Spey, 1979
Murder and Mystery in the Highlands, 1977
Victorian & Edwardian Highlands in Old Photographs, 1976
The Highlands and Islands, 1974
The Uists and Barra, 1974
St. Kilda, 1970
Harris Tweed, 1969
Harris and Lewis, 1968

The Supernatural Highlands

FRANCIS THOMPSON

Luath Press Limited
EDINBURGH
www.luath.co.uk

First published by Robert Hale & Company, London 1976
This edition 1997

Full details of other books currently available from Luath
are set out on the final pages of this book.

The author and publishers acknowledge with grateful thanks
the permission of the Trustees of the late Alexander Carmichael
and the Directors of the Scottish Academic Press, Edinburgh,
to quote from Carmina Gadelica extracts on
pp 83, 113, 132 and poems on pp 134-144.

This book is made from low chlorine pulps produced in
a low energy, low emission manner from renewable
forests and from recycled materials, the latter
comprising at least 50% of the pulps used.

Printed and bound by
Gwasg Dinefwr Press Ltd., Llandybie

Cover Image – The Callanish Stones on the Isle of Lewis,
said to be the petrified bodies of giants who refused
to be baptised by St. Kieran. Photo by David Paterson.

Contents

PREFACE		7
INTRODUCTION		9
CHAPTER 1	Witchcraft	14
CHAPTER 2	The Evil Eye	35
CHAPTER 3	Second Sight	45
CHAPTER 4	Ghosts	67
CHAPTER 5	Functional Folklore	75
CHAPTER 6	Seasonal Lore	88
CHAPTER 7	Supernatural Beings	101
CHAPTER 8	The Power of Words	134
BIBLIOGRAPHY		145
INDEX		152

Preface

SINCE THE FIRST APPEARANCE of this book, the Highlands and Islands of Scotland have been placed under a microscope. Significant sea-changes have occurred in attitudes towards social and economic aspects of the region. New primary sources of historical research have given rise to a need for re-assessment of the events of the past to generate a new understanding of many of the traumatic incidents which litter the pages of Highland history. One might think that the subject of this book would have remained fixed in its own aspic. But even in this area of folk belief and tradition, new insights into the manner in which life was played out in the past have promised a new understanding of a community which relied heavily on the experience and practical knowledge of those community members who were known as tradition-bearers.

In one particular, recent concern at the disappearance of plant species has thrown into relief the fact that these same species do contain substances which have a potential for the abatement of and cure for many of the illnesses affecting humans. That the medical profession now tends to accept that what were once called old-wives' tales have a basis in reality means that there is still a future for what might be described as functional folklore. Certainly what has transpired from research over the past two decades is a realisation that the close-knit and relatively simple lives of the people of the Highlands and Islands were well-bedded in proven means to survive the problems of living in their uncertain times.

Even topics such as the 'second sight' have recently been given a fresh approach, comparing its existence in the Highlands with its counterparts in other countries as far away as Japan. A seminar held in Edinburgh a few years ago attracted a number of delegates to discuss the subject. They agreed that those whose lives were more governed by natural events still retained the ability to foresee the future. Television producers have no problem in devising programmes based on the other dimensions which seem to impact on modern life and living.

On one level this book can be read as a simple introduction to the way of life of the rural and island communities of the Highlands and Islands of yesteryear and in the more recent past. On another level the reader can take the opportunity to obtain new and different sight-lines which might throw new shafts of light into areas of belief which were once dismissed as folklore, or even classed as superstition and therefore not worth the coin.

Francis Thompson,
June 1997

Introduction

IT WAS SCOTS AUTHOR John Buchan who warned that, while new days bring new ways, a land in the turmoil of change should be aware of "casting aside as provincial and antiquated the things that belong to the very core and essence of its being". The people of any nation indeed lose sight of their traditional heritage at their peril; and while folk tradition might be a small part of our heritage, it may well be that if we do not know that heritage, we do not quite know ourselves. Buchan's statement is no less true for the Scottish Highlands and Islands, which have fortunately remained a significant repository for all the facets of a folk culture. It has a standing of at least two millennia and is set firmly and securely in a contemporary context which is increasingly recognising the worth of the past to satisfy the needs for roots and identity in a world which imposes on the individual the idea that conformity is the ultimate goal in life. The culture is still strongly Gaelic-based, despite the fact that much of the mainland Highlands has now become bilingual and largely English-speaking. The rhythms, too, of Highland life still beat to an older time, particularly on the west coastal parts of the region and, more especially, in the Outer Hebrides.

To claim for a European folk-culture that its roots go back some two thousand years might seem to emanate from unbounded enthusiasm, considering that up to the end of the last century or so the vehicle for the transmission of the culture was oral tradition, and that the literary medium is really a Johnny-come-lately. But the claim can be substantiated by stating that the Gaelic-based culture of the region is also derived from Celtic origins—and these go back to the fifth century B.C. There exists a considerable volume of material about the Celts in the ancient literature of Ireland—despite the attempts of the Church at expurgation. This material comprises many mythological tracts which survive in the guise of history; they contain the names of numerous deities, principal festivals, and accounts of the activities of the Druids. Echoes of these appear as muted murmurings in the folk traditions, tales and customs of Scotland, Ireland, Wales, Cornwall, Man and Brittany—the six Celtic domains of Europe which, despite centuries of subjugation by colonialists, still display the characteristic traits of the Celt.

T. G. E. Powell, in his book *The Celts*, states that the Celts were more concerned with magic and the observances of ritual than with organised religion, and that, even though there existed a Celtic pantheon, this was in no way as organised as the Greek and Roman counterparts. It is this which must be borne in mind when approaching the 'Supernatural Highlands'; for even when there is a strong grafted skin of Christian religion to be found laid securely over the items of folklore and tradition, this skin can in fact be peeled away to reveal an older bedrock. Then, as now in the present corpus of Highland folklore, life was regulated by the two principal seasons: warm and cold. These were further subdivided so that four festivals marked the turning-points of each twelvemonth. The greatest festival was Samhainn, celebrated, in terms of the modern calendar, on 1 November, with its 'eve' being the most significant part of the festival. Samhainn marked the end of one year and the beginning of the next—a starting point in a pastoralist rather than an agrarian cycle. It marked the end of the grazing season and the herding of animals to be separated either for breeding or for slaughter. The real significance of Samhainn was its magical context: it ensured the renewal of earthly prosperity and the success of the community. The Festival of Beltane, held on 1 May, marked the beginning of the warm season and was also an essentially pastoralist festival, when the cattle were driven to open grazing. A particular feature was the lighting of two great fires between which cattle were driven, to protect them from disease; the ritual was supervised by Druids.

The other two festivals were Imbolc (1 February) and Lugnasad (1 August). The former marked the beginning of lactation in ewes and it corresponds to the Feast of St Brigit in the Christian calendar. While sheep possessed no particular status, as did other animals in the Celtic bestiary, they provided wool which was an important element in Celtic domestic economy. Lugnasad is unusual in that it is more concerned with agrarian activity—the harvesting of crops. It marked the success of ritual and observances undertaken to ensure the success of crops, rather than an occasion for thanksgiving. In the world of the Celtic supernatural, and this is also evident in the supernatural Highlands, the continued prosperity of the community depended on the careful observance of ritual, based on magic, and not on supplication; this latter feature of later tradition seems to have been introduced as the result of 'Christianising' influences attempting to cover ancient beliefs with a new ideological paint.

In the Celtic world, the chief practitioner of magic and ritual was the Druid. The word is derived from Continental Celtic, through Greek and Latin texts. As a word it originates from roots meaning "knowledge of the oak": assuming that the oak was the symbol of deity, such knowledge was appropriate to those who operated in a supernatural domain and who were able, on behalf of others, to mediate between the plain man in the community and the shadowy figures who inhabited the world of the unknown. The Druid was able to 'see' these figures and to communicate with them through the medium of the trance or some stimulated inspiration. That the Druid was something more than a 'religious' must also be considered; his vast store of knowledge, his ability to operate on elevated mental planes, to use hypnotism, thought transference, auto-suggestion, telekinesis, telepathy and the like, might go some way to explain the existence in the folklore of Celtic countries of such 'supermen' of whom Merlin is a popular example. In our world of humans where so much emphasis is placed on the storage of knowledge in the written word and in electronic vaults, it is perhaps hard to accept that the human mind can acquire, process and store a vast amount of knowledge and information, can rationalise, evaluate and compare, and is capable of instant 'information retrieval'. Yet, it has been the experience of folklorists in Scotland and Ireland in recent times to encounter men and women who could recite tales continuously for days and divulge a mass of other folk information besides; the archives of the School of Scottish Studies in Edinburgh stand witness to these tradition-bearers of Scotland. Perhaps they are a feature of so-called primitive and unsophisticated societies, where minds are uncluttered by the usual things which occupy the urban mind. If so, then this book is an apt medium through which to offer thanks to those who have made it possible for others to tune in and synchronise with such a wealth of the past in the present. The mechanism of oral learning is largely that of continuous repetition by chanting simple verse or alliterative prose forms. The rhythm may induce a semi-ecstatic state during which, over a period of years, the mind can absorb a great body of material. Caesar's description of the training of the Druids' pupils in many verses over the years makes some sense. He, however, misunderstood the Druids' scant regard for written texts; it was not just a matter of maintaining secrecy: writing did not have the necessary ritual acceptance and was not hallowed by ancient usage. Thus the Druid in the Celtic community justified his status, position and role as a true fount of knowledge on which the community depended for its successful continuity into the future.

The foregoing is a brief but necessary introduction to the subject of this book. 'Folklore' is a topic which so easily becomes 'superstition', a degeneration which detracts greatly from the real import of folk tradition, and it is only when one approaches the subject with some rationale that one can begin to appreciate the real stuff of which a people are made. Those who look for 'whimsy' will be disappointed; those who seek roots, reasons and rationale will, perhaps, feel that this attempt to shed a fresh light on Highland folklore has been justified, even though the present state of knowledge of the 'supernatural' is still embryonic. The book might be regarded as a step into the unknown —as a faltering pace taken across a threshold-stone of unknown dimension. The author claims no more for the work than this, and hopes that he may be joined by others who, while reserving their own rights to query and interpret, might help to take a second step into those domains of the supernatural world of 'supernature' which at present require mind-stretching and unorthodox techniques before one can come to terms with it, however uneasy these terms might be.

Four-square people might argue that to make a distinction between folklore and superstition is to split a hair from the same dog's tail; and on that basis argue that the 'supernatural Highlands' is synonymous with the 'superstitious Highlands'. However, the author claims that there is a difference. There are many definitions of 'folklore'. Webster's Dictionary lists no fewer than fifteen definitions from which one can make a choice. The definition nearest the mark is that folklore is the survival of thought and ways of life of former times. This folklore is knowledge, mostly preserved by oral transmission and, generally, divorced from the rationally based knowledge of educated classes of people. This is not to say that those who believed in folklore were not educated, but that the two types of knowledge served different purposes for different people. We are largely conditioned by the mental climate of our times and locality. Nowadays we tend to approach most situations which we meet with a rationalistic cast of mind. But this veneer can crack from side to side whenever we are faced with times of emotion or uncertainty. What many fail to realise is that not only has past folklore survived in different guises to this very day and hour, but that new folklore is growing branches and new twigs on very old stock. Folklore is as old as Eden and as young as the unborn tomorrow; and those who deny that they subscribe to folklore beliefs, fault themselves in their action and thoughts.

'Superstition' derives from the Latin *super* (above) and *stare* (to stand), to offer a word which means standing over, or survival. It really describes an irrational or credulous attitude towards magico-religious beliefs and practices of a civilised community, long after these primitive ideas and customs have been abandoned by the more sophisticated sections of society. Many superstitions are often found to be contradictory and indeterminate in character. This is because they are an unorganised collection of cult customs and beliefs which survived from practices and ideas dropped long ago into a limbo and either forgotten or disowned. But in times of stress, when the element of chance is predominant, and security is very uncertain, superstitions recur, with little or no knowledge generally of what really lies behind the things said or done to avert disaster. They are thought to 'work', which is to say that they bring luck or avert misfortune. And this is all that matters to the person reverting to the old practice of some superstitious saying or deed. Thus actions are performed, spells are uttered, as they were in times past, in the hope of confidence and success, and with a blind faith in the *modus operandi*.

Throughout most of this book I have suggested that we look afresh at some of the aspects of Highland folklore to see if there are grounds for changing our stance to obtain a new and different sight-line which would throw a shaft of new light into an otherwise dark area, ignored because of its association with superstition. Even the acceptance that "there is something in it" is a half-step, a half-belief indicating the need for an open mind on many topics presented herein—at least until the world of science admits that the world as we know it is not four-square but is multi-faceted and has dimensions only sensed as yet.

Popular and controversial writers such as T. C. Lethbridge and Erich van Däniken have posed problems for the practitioners and high priests of knowledge in our present-day world. The accepted fact of second sight is only one area in which these academics find themselves stumped. It is not asking too much for a re-orientation of sight-lines in science to take in the unknown, if only to add an extra dimension of interest to life and living, or even to offer new horizons to replace those which are now covered in the haze of ignorance and unconcern. One final point to introduce this book. It is an instance of magical belief living on into our scientific age which occurred in one of the Scottish islands where some members of the Edinburgh School of Scottish Studies went to look at a stone where people suffering from toothache used to knock in a nail: the pain went away into the stone with the nail. National Health dentists are now available on the island, but some of the nail-heads seen sticking out, exposed to the elements, were still bright—and hardly touched by rust . . .

CHAPTER I

Witchcraft

THE CORPUS OF PRACTICES and beliefs known as witchcraft extends
back to a time which pre-dates the origins of many of the present
major religions of the world. Like these other religions it has a history
of persecution, attenuation, schisms and growth—and survives today
in a number of forms. The rise in general public interest in various
occult forms in the past decade or so has fixed the attention of those
who had hitherto regarded witchcraft as part of a rather tenuous folk
belief which was highlighted by two important points: first, that there
was remarkably little persecution of witches and magicians during the
earlier Middle Ages, with a particularly notable decline around the ninth
and tenth centuries; and, secondly, that by the end of the fifteenth
century, during the Renaissance, the legal and theological crime of
witchcraft had been moulded into a finished form. Some scholars have
seen historical witchcraft as the consequence of the long age of despair
in medieval Europe: as a form of serf response to the otherwise unbear-
able despair of their condition, and as a kind of communion of revolt
acted out at night against the lord of the manor and his church.

By the end of the nineteenth century a generation of rationalists
and positivists appeared to react against the romantic ideas of witchcraft propounded by Sir Walter Scott; they were firmly sceptical about
the historical reality of the cult, both past and contemporary. This
stance and attitude was countered rigorously, principally by the late Dr
Margaret Murray, whose central thesis was that 'ritual' (as opposed
to 'operational' or black magic) witchcraft was really the survival in
Europe of an ancient fertility cult based on the worship of Diana. The
debate about witchcraft continues to generate a great deal of heat and
little light, except that produced by historical research into the prelude
to the witch burnings of the sixteenth and seventeenth centuries. This
research has indicated that many of the accusations of witchcraft were
in fact based deep in antiquity, to the time when the early Christian
communities were the object of strange suspicions and charges. Then
occurred the demonisation of medieval heretics, such as the Waldensians and the Fraticelli, a grouping derived from the original confraternity

founded by St Francis. The crushing of the Knights Templar was achieved by accusations charged full with witchcraft. All these events, given slow but substantial credence through the ensuing centuries, placed in the popular mind, and that of organised religion, the idea that a society of witches existed in Europe. Thus, from the time the first person was tried formally for practising ritual magic (Pope Boniface VIII who was tried posthumously in 1310–11) until the great witch hunt, there was a gradual build-up of hysteria among the common folk, a tool which those in high places were not slow to pick up and use for their own ends.

The great witch hunt of Europe is only now beginning to be studied in detail. It was not, in the main, a cynical operation. Financial greed and conscious sadism, though by no means lacking in all cases, did not supply the main driving force—that was supplied by misplaced religious zeal. Torture, when it was used, was not only legitimate but divinely required. The witch, being regarded as not merely an ally of the Devil but being in the grip of a demon, had to be subjected to torture to break that grip. The battle, fought in the torture chamber, was a fight between God and the Devil for the witch's own soul: a witch who confessed and perished in the flames had at least a chance of purging his or her guilt and achieving salvation. It was generally held that God would give an innocent person enough strength to withstand any amount of torture. In fact, this belief was given credence by the fact that an estimated one in ten of those tortured held out and were actually set free. The witch hunt can be taken as a supreme example of a massive killing of innocent people by a bureaucracy acting in accordance with beliefs which, unknown or rejected in earlier centuries, had come to be taken for granted, as self-evident truths. It is a perfect illustration of how the human imagination can build up a stereotype and yet be reluctant to question the validity of the stereotype once it is generally accepted. The amount of collusion, between peasantry, the trade class, the religionists, and the aristocracy and the magistrates, to stage witch trials, is unknown, but was no doubt significant. At the present time, superficial attempts by the TV media to 'expose' the cult, aided and abetted by the two-penny-coloured magazines, based on a sexually-entertaining basis, do nothing but confuse the whole issue; the true bases of contemporary belief and practice in witchcraft are still obscure. Even a definition as to what witchcraft really entertains within its wide compass is in debate. Some suppose that it is the worship of the Great Horned God; others opine that the religion is rooted in some folk-society structure which requires that one or more persons in a community act as propitiators for the rest, to effect, whether they have real powers or not, the best for their fellows in terms of material benefit and freedom from real or imaginary evil influences.

It has also been suggested that witchcraft should be understood primarily as a manifestation of social conflict: between monastic orders and their superficially Christian flocks in the Middle Ages, between Protestants and Catholics, and, ultimately, between lawyers or clergy and educated laymen. It was also associated with rural poverty in areas normally inaccessible and remote from centres of population, areas which were breeding grounds for variations of orthodox religious beliefs. These areas in fact have often been proved to have a greater resistance to the introduction of new orthodoxies and again and again have to be won back to sound religion. Such poor soil indeed offered little return for churches and their missionaries. We see this situation in England, where the north and the west, "the dark corners of the realm", had to be re-evangelised by Puritan missionaries a century after the Reformation; and also in Scotland, where the Highlands relapsed into "paganism' and required rescue operations to be mounted by the new Puritan movement of the eighteenth century. Gospel carried into the unfeudal, half-Christian societies of remote parts inevitably, in that different world, found that its success was always transitory: that the ancient habits of thought and practice always reasserted themselves, that social incompatibility clothed itself in religious heresy; and that when formal heresy had been silenced or burnt out, the same fundamental incompatibility took, or seemed to take, another form. The old rural superstition, which had seemed harmless enough in the interstices of known society, assumed a more dangerous character when it was discovered, in strange and exaggerated form, among the barely subdued 'heretics' of the remote areas. Thanks to that social gulf, that social unassimilability, witchcraft became heresy.

The witch panic which swept Europe in the sixteenth and seventeenth centuries sorely affected Scotland, where ministers of religion joined on the side of intolerance, injustice and superstition to become party to what can only be termed as judicial murder. The final accolade was the enhancement of the witch-hunt cult into a distinct canon or arbitrary faith in which the whole industry of witch-hunting became an activity of political significance and social power, in which humanity and common sense played no part and in which autocracy and superstition became the creed of the moment. One cannot but look at the whole record of witch persecution and ask who really were the witches and who the judges and executioners. In the historical event the witches were, in too many cases, the aged, the weak, the deformed, the lame, the blind and the mentally ill—unfortunate beings who, having become the object of a neighbour's malice, jealousy or spite, were thrown into an ordeal which tested them to the limit and then demanded the final payment of death, as an act of shriving the soul of taint. The judges and executioners of these unfortunates were the wisest, the greatest and the most learned of their times, distinguished above their fellows for knowledge and intelligence: ministers of the religions, the law, kings, princes and nobles.

The greatest pity was due to those who, by reason of the lore of healing they possessed, carried over faithfully on behalf of their fellows, from the experiences of previous generations—the 'white' witches of today—suffered the indiscriminate attentions of witch-hunters and witchfinders who cared not that a community might lose its only access to medical aid and knowledge; doctors were the exception rather than the commonplace provision in remote areas. Fortunately in the Highlands, perhaps because of the region's comparative inaccessibility, or perhaps again because of the different nature of the fundamental and elemental beliefs of Highlanders who saw in nature the natural phenomenon rather than the miraculous, the witch was more a figure of legend, mythology and the folktale, rather than a reality to be feared, hated and persecuted. The proximity of the Highland lifestyle to nature, or even where this was an uneasy juxtaposition, evolved a healthy respect which prevented, and indeed probably resented, the attitude of callousness as was displayed in the rest of Scotland, and in the more accessible parts of the Highland region.

The evidence on the Highland witches is that while they have many similar points of contact, conduct and attitude with their sisters in the Scottish south, there is, comparatively, very little of the repulsive element in their character. Tales regarding the witches in the Highlands make no mention of such aliens as the incubus, the succubus, nor of midnight meetings, Sabbats, dancing with the Devil and other aspects so common in other areas of Scotland, England and Europe. Neither do we hear of Highland witches riding through the air on broomsticks nor raising the dead; where this does occur it is either legend or an importation. Many witches were, of course, credited with powers obtained from the Devil, so that they could, for instance, raise winds favourable or otherwise for ships, transport themselves from place to place, by disintegration to reappear in other places, and generally use their powers for evil purposes, at the behest of those who were willing to pay the right price. Unless payment was given a Highland witch was often powerless to satisfy the payer's requirements. Indeed, it is surprising, and this is a general observation, that if one considers the power witches were supposed to possess, how they managed to remain in indigent circumstances, often all of their lives. One explanation is that though they could do things for others they were powerless to help themselves or improve their material well-being. This, however, is not the claim of a number of modern witches, such as the male witch in California who is reputed to be a millionaire because of the astute and dubious use of his knowledge of black arts and possibly blacker talents for duplicity and preying on the well-heeled credulous.

One indication of the background and nature of the Highland witch type is seen in the Gaelic word *buidseach*; this is identical in meaning with the English word 'witch', a word which it resembles phonetically. The word, when used in Gaelic, was applied to both 'black' and 'white' witches, whether they were credited with devilish activity or were honest and harmless practitioners of sorcery "whom our custom and country doth call wise men and wise women" (Cotta, *Short Discovery of Unobserved Dangers*, 1612). But while in Gaelic there are no words corresponding to black and white witches, the distinction between types and their functions and respective powers was widely known; it was common to apply the word *buidseach* to those who could do harm. These raised storms, drowned people, took the milk from cows and the substance from food. White witches, on the other hand, cured by magic charms, or by the application of the known curative properties of plants, diseases in man and beast, bestowed luck, warded off dangers, both real and imaginary, and secured various benefits for their clients. In fact, they would have been the first to resent any accusation that they were dabblers in witchcraft. Indeed, many of their supplications for cures were made by appeals to saints and the persons of the Holy Trinity. In many cases, their 'witchcraft' was an extension of diluted religious beliefs, severely attenuated because of neglect by the orthodox Church. The machinery by which the Highland white witch secured blessings for humanity consisted of the recitation of rhymes and incantations, the performance of rites and ceremonies, the use of plants and stones of virtue, supposedly possessing occult powers, and the observance of propitious seasons and so on. In modern times the functions and powers of these white witches would be based on 'superstition'.

Superstition in Scotland seems to stem from the nation's Celtic origins—derived from the natural recognition of those aspects of life, intangible as they were, influenced the material web of lifestyles of both individual and community, to such an extent that the 'unknown', as these tangibles often were, developed into something to be feared, particularly by those whose minds were riddled with trouble; or revered by those whose minds had the key to gain access to the mental planes of peace, solace and solitude that these areas offered.

In the Highlands, where the very lay of the land lent itself to thoughts of the beings which might populate the lonely glens, the deep lochs, the rivers and streams, there were many whose minds were centred on such beings as the Kelpie, ready to rush out from river banks to catch unwary travellers. The fatal Banshee heralded death and misfortune. But to offset these evil spirits were the gentler species whose relationship with the human race was more than benevolent. However, it is when we examine the position of the witch in the community that we see the considerable difference in attitudes towards the function of witchcraft in the lowland south—and we see the Highlands in a light of tolerance which could well have been copied elsewhere, but which 'elsewhere' was unable to do simply because of increasing sophistication. This increase in knowledge, whatever that knowledge was worth, reduced the relevance of superstition, witchcraft and the like to a datum of everyday things and generated an unholy superstition which caused the cruel deaths of many innocents; it eventually became a scapegoat for personal greed and ambition. In the Highlands, however, where the people were closer to nature and, perhaps, understood, or at least tolerated, witches with a charitable or quasi-Christian kindness, there were few instances of the merciless hunts for witches which were so characteristic of almost the whole of the rest of Europe.

There were four areas of operation by the white witch: Eolas (knowledge) for the cure of disease; Oradh (gilding) for securing gifts and graces; Sian or Seun (charm) for protection from danger; and Soisgeal (Gospel) for weak minds.

Eolas was also known as Teagasg (teaching) and was a charm for the cure of sickness in man or beast. It generally consisted of a rhyme, muttered over the sick person, and over the water to be drunk by, or sprinkled over, the sick animal. To render it more impressive, its use was accompanied by some small ceremonies, such as making the sign of the cross, making up mysterious parti-coloured threads, getting particular kinds of water on particular days or times of the day, dipping stones of virtue (with supposed occult powers). Whatever could be said for the Eolas, if it did not cure, it certainly did not kill. Eolas was used for illnesses of a transitory nature: toothache, bruises, sprains, eye sties and the like.

Second in popularity was the securing of protection for both man and beast from particular occult dangers, such as being taken away by an enemy, being drowned, or struck by a sword, bullet or arrow in battle. The Seun (Scot: *sain*) consisted of rhymes, parti-coloured threads, or plants. It was said over cows and sheep when leaving them to their own devices for the night; put round the necks of infants; given by a fairy mistress (*leannan sith*)to her mortal lover; sewn by a mother into the clothes of a son about to leave the house; or given to a young lass whose lover was soon to go into battle. Highland tales abound in instances of men returned from fierce fighting unscathed by bullet and sword.

The Soisgeul was a charm intended to strengthen the weak mind so that grace might be conferred on a poor soul. It consisted of a green string, kept in the mouth while the charm was muttered, then secured to the right shoulder of the person being charmed. The ceremony was performed on a Thursday or Sunday to have maximum effect. Often a verse of Scripture, hymn, or some good words, obtained from a priest, were written down and sewn into the clothes to prevent the occurrence of weakness of mind, and to protect against spite.

Black witchcraft for the prosecution of an evil purpose was not unknown, however; far from it. But accepting it as part of life and living, as we do today the presence of vandals and the bombing of innocent people, the black witch was regarded with fear on account of the possible influence he or she might have over others. There was the unlimited influence of the curse; the sin and mischief to be wrought by charm and spell; the power of casting sickness, blight on the corn and murrain on beasts; and there was the strength of the evil eye which could contain a curse in a greeting, or radiate a malice with such effect that a creature could be killed at a glance. On the other hand, white witchcraft was respected for the good it did in a community; those responsible for it held a high place in the esteem of the people.

Thomas Pickering, in his *Discourse of the Damned Art of Witchcraft*, printed in 1610, says:

> Of witches there be two sorts, the bad witch and the good witch; for so they are commonly called. The bad witch is he or she that hath consulted in league with the Deuill; to use his helpe for the doing of hurte onely, so as to strike and annoy the bodies of men, women, children, cattell, with diseases and with death itselfe; so likewise to rause tempests by sea and by land, &c. This is commonly called the binding witch.
>
> The good witch is he or shee that by consent in a league with the Dueill doth use his helpe for the doing of good onely. This cannot hurte, torment, curse, or kill, but onely heale and cure the hurt inflicted upone men or cattell by badde witches. For as they can doe no good but onely hurt; so this can doe no hurt but good onely. And this is that order which the Dueill hath set in his kingdome, appointing to severall persons their severall offices and charges. And the Good Witch is commonly called the Unbinding Witch.

Until the end of the sixteenth century, trials for witchcraft in Scotland were few, even though laws, dating back to the reign of Kenneth I, made provision for the burning of sorcerers; the Duffus case shows that organised witchcraft was practised and believed long before it appeared south of the Border. In common with England, the early trials in Scotland charged witchcraft for political ends, as is evidenced in the classic politically oriented case of the Earl of Mar, Lady Glamis and Lady Foulis. About the middle of the sixteenth century it became a statutory offence to consort with a witch, even for beneficent sorcery and fortune-telling. After this the previous trickle of witch trials became a flood. King James VI was in many ways responsible for placing witchcraft at the disposal of those who wished harm to their neighbours, for all kinds of ends. The Aberdeen Witches trial, for instance, in 1597, was stimulated by the king's *Demonologie* (1597). The result of this case affected a wide spectrum of people, and particularly those in rural communities who were often resorted to for concoctions of herbal cures and natural remedies. Not only this, but the intense interest created in the trial sparked off a pathological interest in witchcraft generally.

By 1662 the bare bones of beliefs in Scottish witchcraft had been exposed, culminating in the Isobel Gowdie trial of that year. This contains some of the clearest references to coven and sabbat and also shows the extent to which European witch customs had infiltrated the Scottish branch of the belief. It took another century before reason prevailed to free Scotland from the curse, not of witchcraft, but of intolerance, injustice and bigotry.

Scottish witches in myth, legend and folktale have a long lineage, going back to the time when St Patrick offended some of them, and the Devil as well, by his uncompromising rigour against them. In revenge they attacked him near Dumbarton. But Patrick, knowing that they could not cross over water, got into a boat and sailed for Ireland. In fury the witches lifted between them a huge rock which they threw after him. They missed the saint but where the rock landed has been known as Dumbarton Rock ever since. Almost six centuries later King Duffus of Scotland was the victim of black witchcraft. A wax image was made of the king which was roasted and basted with a poison. As if this were not enough, the witches involved made enchantments to deprive the king of sleep. Despite the close attentions of royal doctors, there was nothing that could be done—until it was discovered that the perpetrators of the king's illness were witches intent on seeking revenge for a wrong he had done them. Soon after the wax image was destroyed the king recovered his health, and condemned the witches to be burnt to death at Forres, in Moray. The image-working was revealed by a young woman in the king's court who had become distraught at the sight of the illness and who confessed that one of the witches was her mother. In later centuries Thomas of Ercildoune, whom the Queen of Fairy loved and kept, and the amazing Sir Michael Scott of Balweary, second to none in power, caught the imagination of Scots. In 1480 it was reported that the young Lady of Mar had given herself up to a loathsome incubus. Half a century later it was the turn of Lady Glamis to fall foul of the growing cult of hatred which took the practice of witchcraft as a useful and all too convenient vehicle for personal enmity towards others.

In Inverness, the first notice of witchcraft in the town records is dated 7 March 1558, when Sandy Macillmertin was judged to be guilty of saying in the open market at Inverness, and in the hearing of witnesses, particularly one Henry Kerr, that his servant had put witchcraft in his net, presumably to increase the catch of salmon. Fourteen years after, on 26 July 1572, Agnes Cuthbert of Inverness had to apologise in church for saying that she had put witchcraft into Christina Dingwall's ale, so that, try as she might, poor Christina "could get no sale for it". The last witchcraft entry is dated April 1662, itemising an occasion when three baillies, two laymen and a minister were ordered to hear and try witches then in ward, to see whether "they will adhere to their former confessions and try what further they will confess". There were, however, many other trials of witches at Inverness, with the inevitable penalty of burning. The punishment invariably took place at the Haugh. It was here, on 2 December 1603, that Donald Moir Macpherson Miller was burnt, after a trial by a jury which found him guilty of using enchantment and "devillish witchcraft". Later a woman witch, well known as "Creibh Mhor", was burnt on the Castle Hill, Inverness.

Just outside the town, the Millburn valley was long regarded as a centre of witchcraft. Many of the poor people of the district lived there in low, bothy-type houses. One day some children playing by the Mill Burn found a clay figure with pins sticking in it and one of them remarked that she had seen her grandmother making such figures. The news of the discovery spread like wildfire and Creibh Mhor, who was the grandmother in question, became the subject of an inquiry and the magistrates of the town applied to the Privy Council in Edinburgh for a commission "to try witches". Both Creibh Mhor and her sister were arrested. The sister could not withstand the subsequent torture and confessed that the clay figure was meant to be a worthy of the town, Cuthbert of Castle Hill. The poor women were eventually sentenced to be burnt at the stake. Creibh Mhor was first for death; when the flames and smoke began to envelop her she cried out to the people standing around for mercy's sake to give her a mouthful of water to quench her thirst. Some sympathetic person ran to get some water and was about to give it to her when he was told that the object of his pity was a witch, on hearing which he promptly emptied the water on to the ground. When Creibh Mhor saw this she cursed them all: "If only I had got a mouthful of that water I would have turned Inverness into a peat bog!"

Her sister, who had confessed in the thought that she might be spared of the burning, saw that there was to be no hope of reprieve and, turning to her guard, said: "Well, well. If I had thought it would come to this there would have been many who wear scarlet cloaks here today." This was a reference to the fact that many of the well-to-do ladies of Inverness were not above consulting the poor women of the bothies at Millburn in the hope that by the practice of witchcraft their hopes and dreams would come to pass, even if someone had to be 'removed' in the process.

Probably it is because there is a Gaelic proverb *Cha tig olc a's teine* (no evil comes out of a fire) that witches were burnt rather than hanged.

Almost half a century previously the Highlands appeared significantly on the witchcraft scene in Scotland when Katherine Ross, Lady Foulis, and her stepson, Hector Munro, were tried on 22 June 1590 for "Witchcraft, Incantation, Sorcery and Poisoning". Katherine Ross was of high rank, both by her own family and that of her husband, the fifteenth Baron of Foulis and Chief of the Clan Munro. She became involved in a strained argument with her stepson, Robert Munro, eldest son of her husband, which reached the stage where she determined to see Robert's death. This possibility opened up a number of options to her, including the advantage that the widow of Robert, once Robert was removed, should marry Lady Foulis's brother, George Ross of Balnagowan; but to achieve this particular objective it was necessary that the current Lady Balnagowan be also removed. The scheme being laid, it then required suitable instruments for its prosecution and progress, and Lady Foulis resorted to witchcraft. She negotiated with several people in the neighbourhood who practised witchcraft, two wizards and a witch known as Lasky Loncart. These people, at the time, were lodged with a Christina Ross Malcolmson. Images of the young Lady Balnagowan and the young Laird of Foulis were made of butter and shot at with elf arrows (flint arrowheads which are relics of past ancestors and which were believed at one time to be fairy weapons). Other images of clay were made, wrapped in linen and buried under a bridge end.

As the article of accusation laid against Lady Foulis relates, it was alleged that there was

> the making of two clay pictures, one for the destruction of the young Lady Balnegowan, and getting them enchanted, and shooting of elf-arrow heads at the said persons; second, for making a stoupfull of poisoned aill for performance of your devillish malice, wherewith ye killed sundry; third, sending a pigfull of poyson to the house where young Foulis was, the carrier whereof falling, and with the fall breaking the pig, and seeing the liquor, tasted it, and dyed immediately; and the grasse which grows where it fell, no

beast will eat of it; fourth, for saying that ye would use all means
that may be had of God in heaven, or the devill in hell, for destroy-
ing Marjory Campbell, Lady Balnagowan, that the laird might
marry Lady Foulis; also hindering a commission that was granted
for tryall of witches, and procuring a suspension thereof, which, if
thou hadst been an honest woman, thou would never have done.

Each of the witches consulted contributed their skills to Lady Foulis.
The 'clay pictures' were made by Christina Ross and Lasky Loncart;
the latter also concocted the "poisoned aill" Another, John MacMillan,
sold Lady Foulis the arrowhead, for "four shillings". Agnes Roy, another
witch, was asked to "speak to the fairies" as to how to bring about the
death of Robert Munro and Lady Balnagowan.

When eventually the deeds of the scheme became known Lady
Foulis fled to Caithness, where she remained in hiding for nearly a year
until she was persuaded to return south for trial The trial itself was an
indictment of the whole public attitude towards witchcraft. Despite
the fact that several of Lady Foulis's co-conspirators had died con-
fessing the whole plot, and though it was common knowledge in the
district that the 'carrier', Lady Foulis's nurse, had tasted the contents
of the jar which had fallen and broken, and died of the result, Lady
Foulis was set free with the verdict: ". . . said Katherine was innocent
and quit of all the points of the indictment".

The witches whom Lady Foulis consulted fared worse. Christina
Ross was burnt for her part in the crime at Chanonry, near Fortrose, a
place later to be the scene in popular memory of the physical destruction of the Brahan Seer. William Macgillimondan, who also suffered
death for the same practices, confessed the acts of poison, and in particular, an attempt to destroy the Chief of Munro.

Lady Foulis's son-in-law, Hector Munro of Foulis, was also
brought to trial for witchcraft practices at the same time, having to
change his role at the trial from prosecutor of his stepmother to
defender of his own life against an accusation that he conspired
to take the life of his brother. This he was alleged to have done by
consulting with some witches in the district, in particular Marion
MacIngarach, and his own foster-mother, Christian Neil Dalyell. The
accusation against Hector Munro was that he had caused George
Munro's death by transferring his illness to the latter by some rather
improbable means. In the event, after a plea of Not Guilty, and appearing before a jury of his friends, Hector Munro was declared not guilty.
In both these trials it was patently obvious that though some lower-
class persons suffered the full penalty of death, those who were the
real architects of the crimes alleged were set free.

The year 1662 in the Highlands presented two important cases of witchcraft, each, in its own way, marking a turning point in the history of witch-hunting.

In the kirk of Auldearn, near Nairn, one Sunday in March 1662, a woman named Isobel Gowdie stood before her accusers and stated:

> As I was going betwixt the towns of Drumdewin and the Heads, I met with the Devill, and there covenanted in a manner with him. And I promised to meet him in the night time in the Kirk of Auldearn. And the first thing I did there that night, I denyed my baptism, and did put one of my hands to the crown of my head, and the other to the sole of my foot, and then renounced all betwixt my two hands over to the Devill.

This declaration is a classic definition of "trafficking with the Devil", the slogan of the witch-hunter. Gowdie's audience included the Sheriff-Depute of Nairn, the Minister of Auldearn, and many of the lairds and men of influence in the district, none of whom would have had any doubts of their religious, moral and legal obligations. If found guilty, Isobel Gowdie would surely burn. As a contemporary observer, Alexander Brodie of Brodie, stated: "The sin of witchcraft and devilry which has prevailed, and cannot be gotten discovered and purged out, Satan having set up his very throne among us."

Against this kind of backcloth, Isobel Gowdie's confessions are unique in their sheer scope and variety. She was seemingly an authority on her subject and was able, and willing, to guide her interrogators through the popular maze of ignorance and misunderstanding that was the world of Satan. "I met with him [the Devil] in the New Yards of Inshoch, and [he] had carnal copulation and dealing with me. He was a meikle, black, roch man, very cold; and I found his nature as cold within me as spring-well-water. Sometimes he had boots and sometimes shoes on his feet; but still his feet are forked and cloven."

Isobel and her fellows made "a picture of clay to destroy the Laird of Park's male children":

> John Taylor brought home the clay in his plaid neuk; his wife [Janet Breadhead] brake it very small, like meal, and sifted it with a sieve, and poured in water among it, in the Devil's name, and wrought it very sore . . . and made of it a picture of the Laird's sons. It had all the parts and marks of a child, such as head, eyes, nose, hands, feet, mouth, and little lips . . . We laid the face of it to the fire, until it shrivelled, and a clear fire round about it, till it was red like a coal. After that we would roast it now and then. Every other day there would be a piece of it well roasted. All the Laird of Park's male children by it are to suffer . . . as well as those that are born and dead already.

Janet Breadhead confirmed much of Isobel Gowdie's confession and descriptions of the activities of the coven. Unless one is prepared to believe in mutually shared hallucinations, the witches in the Auldearn area actually did participate in a wide range of mischievous—and murderous—practices.

All that is really known about Isobel Gowdie is that she was "spouse to John Gilbert in Lochloy". The name is not at all common to the area; it is derived from the Scots 'gowd', or gold. From the energy and the colour in her confessions she was no hag but a young woman. There is a tradition that she was the daughter of an impoverished lawyer whose reduced financial straits caused him to marry off his girl to a surly farmer. Whatever her origins, it was a fact that the kirk elders, baillies, lairds and others had struck a rich vein of evil and they persisted in their inquiries until each last drop of information had been extracted. On four separate occasions Mistress Gilbert repeated and amplified her confessions and one can read from the record where the questionings led, from the gathering of names to the detailing of the practices and the rituals:

> We met in the Kirkyard of Nairn, and we raised an unchristened child out of its grave; and at the end of Broadley's corn-field-land, just opposite to the Mill of Nairn, we took the said child, with the nails of our fingers and toes, pickles of all sorts of grain, and blades of kail, and hacked them all very small, mixed together. And did put a part thereof among the muck-heaps of Broadley's lands, and thereby took away the fruit of his corns.

Though it was stated in the records that Isobel Gowdie spoke her confessions voluntarily and without any persuasion, it may well be that the threat of boots, thumbikins and irons, cold, hunger, racking and the like had some effect. On the other hand, if Isobel Gowdie was of a psychopathic nature she may not have known, or cared, about her actions. On 10 July 1662, the Privy Council granted a Commission for the trial of Isobel Gowdie and Janet Breadhead. But no record of the trial or its outcome has come to light. In November of the same year two witches were burnt at Elgin, and in the following May two more were burnt at Forres; others charged at Nairn and at Inverness were finally freed. Gowdie's fame lives on in the words 'coven' and 'hattock', which words were used by her first.

The year 1662 saw another example of witch-hunting which had a dramatic climax. A certain lowlander called Paterson with a reputation behind him of being a successful witch-finder was invited to the little parish church of Wardlaw, Kirkhill, near Inverness to "prick fourteen women and one man", all MacLeans and accused of witchcraft by the Chisholm of Comar; another four women, accused by Alexander Fraser, Chamberlain of the whisky-distilling parish of Ferintosh, Black Isle, were also to receive Paterson's attentions. When he and his two servants arrived at Kirkhill, he ordered the heads of the prisoners to be shaved. He then mixed all the hair and, for some reason known only to himself, buried the mass in a stone dyke surrounding the kirkyard. What followed may well have been an early form of hypnotism: he rubbed his victim's body all over with his hands and then thrust a long brass pin deep into the flesh. Strangely the accused very often felt nothing and could not find the pin, when told to remove it. This was proof that the pricker had discovered a "devil's spot" and that the victim was certainly a witch. Paterson, however, mixed sadism with his profession: a witch was pricked again and again until the body was so bloated and pained that for the sake of relief from the torture the victim would willingly confess.

During the Kirkhill pricking, Paterson was discovered to be no man, but a woman, and she left the area in great haste. The fact that the pricker was an imposter, however, made no difference to the evidence and the MacLeans were all sent to be confined to the Tolbooth in Inverness. Meanwhile the true facts behind the accusation were revealed: the Chisholm had resorted to charges of witchcraft to remove his MacLean tenants from his Strathglass lands, which they had farmed for three centuries. Having no legal way to evict his tenants he took the most common way out. The prisoners had, by good fortune, the interest of Sir Allan MacLean of Duart in Mull, the Chief of MacLean. He petitioned the Privy Council for justice which was eventually done . . . but not before the prisoners had been tortured "by waking, hanging by the thumbs, holding the soles of the feet to fire, burning, drawing of them by a horse's tail" and worse, so that one died, one went mad, and all confessed.

In July 1699 Ross-shire contributed its share of luckless creatures who were reported as being guilty of the "diabolical crimes and charms of witchcraft". By the end of January 1700, two of them had confessed, and were sentenced to such arbitrary punishment as a committee thought proper. In an observation of this case, Robert Chambers remarks: "This is the first appearance of an inclination in the central authorities to take mild views of witchcraft." By 1718 witches seemed to be in decline. Either they were relegated to their former status in communities as "mad old wives", or persons with a power to help in ailments, or the public belief in witchcraft had been spent, regarding the whole subject as rank superstition. No trials of any note occupied the attentions of the law and common folk until the plague of cats in Caithness.

This case concerned one Margaret Nin-Gilbert, in 1718. This woman had a friend, a Margaret Olsen, who was reputed to "behave wickedly". The latter had been turned out of her house by a Mr Fraser who replaced her as tenant with a William Montgomerie. Resenting this action of Fraser's, Olsen turned to her friend, known locally as a witch, and asked her help to harm Fraser. At first Nin-Gilbert said that as Fraser was a gentleman of rank she had no power over him, nor indeed had she any inclination to harm the man. But Olsen prevailed and they both tried to influence Fraser one night when he was crossing a bridge. Later, on being questioned, Fraser said he remembered perfectly "his horse making a great adoe at that place but that by the Lord's goodness he had escaped". Finding that they had no power over Fraser, the two women turned their attention to the new tenant Montgomerie, a mason. He found that his house became suddenly infested with cats, so much so that it became unsafe for him and his family to stay there. He himself was working away from home when the cats appeared and his wife sent no fewer than five messages asking him to return. Montgomerie's servant left suddenly, claiming that five of the cats had come into her room one night to sit by her fireside where she was alone, and began speaking to each other in human but unintelligible voices. Montgomerie returned home to do battle with the feline enemies. After some encounters in which the cats came off worse, a petition presented to the Sheriff-Depute of Caithness to question some persons in the district "of bad fame" who might be the cause of his trouble. Eventually it came to light that Margaret Nin-Gilbert was seen by one of her neighbours "to drop at her own door one of her leggs from the midle, and she, being under bad fame for witchcraft, the leg", black and putrified, was brought before the Sheriff-Depute". After interrogation, Nin-Gilbert confessed that she was under compact with the Devil, and also said that she had invaded Montgomerie's house as a cat and he had attacked her, wounding her in the leg. She encompassed her friend Margaret Olsen and four other women in her confessions. She died in prison. The others died by hanging and burning.

Four years later, in 1722, Janet Horne, an old woman living in the parish of Loth, Sutherland, was brought before the court accused of various acts of witchcraft. In particular there was a charge that she had transformed her daughter into a pony, which the Devil had shod, making the young woman lame in both her hands and feet for ever after, and had ridden upon her to a sabbat.

The jury brought in a verdict of guilty, and Captain David Ross, the Sheriff-Depute, pronounced sentence of death. The old woman was executed at Dornoch; and it is said that after she was brought to the place of execution, as the weather was very severe, she sat by the fire that had been prepared to consume her "very composedly", while the other instruments of death were being prepared. The daughter was acquitted, as being an unwilling victim of her mother's witchcraft. She transmitted to her son, who was born some years later, the lameness of the hands and feet from which she suffered as the result of the Devil's shoeing.

In 1726, Woodrow notes "some pretty odd accounts of witches", had from a couple of Ross-shire men, but fails to give us very accurate details, save only that one of them at her death "confessed that they had, by sorcery, taken away the sight of one of the eyes of an Episcopal minister, who lost the sight of his eye upon a sudden, and could give no reason for it".

In 1736 the Act Anentis Witchcraft was repealed, to bring the law in Scotland in line with that in England (the last execution for witchcraft in England took place in 1682, when three women were hanged at Exeter). But belief in the delusion died hard, and especially among the seceders from the Established Church of Scotland. In their Annual Confession of National and Personal Sins, printed in an Act of their Associate Presbytery, for the year 1743, they enumerated the Act of Queen Anne's Parliament for tolerating the Episcopal Religion in Scotland; the Act for Adjourning the Court of Session during the Christmas holidays; and also the Penal Statutes against witches, repealed by Parliament, contrary to the Law of God. In 1738 a man was hanged in Sutherland for killing a witch with a spade. He pled that when he attacked her she was in the form of a hare, but this plea did not avail him. In this case a candle was blown out before the sentence of death was pronounced, to herald the last execution in that county of Scotland.

But the spectre of witchcraft was still in evidence in the popular mind twelve years later. In 1750 women alleged to be witches were "cut above the breath" to prevent their doing harm. The Presbytery of Tain found itself having to deal with three men who one night dragged a woman and her daughter out of bed, laid them on the floor and, while two of the men held them down, the third "scored and cut their foreheads with an iron tool calling them witches". The men also forced their victims not to reveal who had assaulted them. The culprits were, however, discovered and were rebuked before the congregations of Alness and Rosskeen, and though one of them believed that the consumption from which he suffered could be cured by this "scoring and cutting", as a counter-charm for his disease, he died at an early age.

An instance of witchcraft appeared in the *Oban Times* in 1880 which was "alleged to be quite true".

> A south countryman went to the Western Isles on one occasion to buy cattle. Going into a certain house at the breakfast hour he

was kindly asked to sit down to breakfast. The man at once complied and among other things placed before him was a quantity of
fresh milk, new from the cow. On tasting the milk, the man,
addressing his hostess, said: "Your milk is spoilt, my good woman;
the fruit is taken from it. " The woman said she was not insensible
of her loss, but that she could not help it; she knew not how to
retain it, and she wished the thieves much good of it. He then
enquired if she knew who did steal it. She answered in the negative, but that she supposed it was one of her neighbours.

"When you go to churn does any person call you to the door?"
he asked. "Indeed, I no sooner begin to make butter than my next
door neighbour calls me to the door for some purpose or other;
but I don't blame her, poor woman, for she is a pious woman, and
is the very last person that would do the like of that." "Be that as
it may, I will give you advice, and that is not to go to the door
when she calls you again. On the contrary, if you refuse her point
blank you will in future have your own butter and milk."

The next time the woman went to church, she resolved to
follow her guest's advice, whatever might be the consequence. The
time came for her to make her butter and no sooner had she sat
down to begin operations than her neighbour came calling at her
door. But the woman paid no attention, despite her neighbour's
cries becoming louder. With a steadfast intention the churn was
operated until the neighbour entered the house and implored to
be set free for "you are tearing the arm off my shoulder".

On hearing this the woman took off the lid of the churn when,
to her great astonishment, she saw the semblance of her neighbour's arm in it. The churn, however, was almost full of butter.
From that day forward she had plenty of good milk and butter.

Highland witches appear in another realm: that of folklore and
legend, a world which they populate and move about with consum-
mate ease and in which the fear of persecution was non-existent. It
was a world which was familiar to the common folk, in the environment of the *ceilidh*, the gatherings on social occasions, and was lodged
firmly in the mainstream of traditional oral story-telling. One of the
tales concerns the witch of Laggan in Badenoch. A hunter who persecuted the whole tribe of witches took shelter from a storm in a
mountain bothy. A cat entered, and the hunter had a difficult task in
trying to pacify his dogs. When the cat saw this it said: "I am a witch
and have taken on this shape, but if you will shelter me I'll give up my
wicked ways." The hunter took pity on her and invited her to sit
down; but she would not do that until he had tied up his hounds, and
she handed him a hair rope with which to do it. He took the hounds to
a corner and, instead of tying up the dogs, wound the rope round a

beam. The cat then sat by the fire and in time changed to a woman known as the Good Wife of Laggan. Then, with fire in her eyes, she said that as he had been the persecutor of her kind, his own hour had now come. The witch flew at the hunter's throat, but not before the dogs, lying low and noiseless in the far corner, jumped to his rescue. Thinking that the dogs were but tied loosely, the witch cried, "Tighten, tighten. " But all that happened was that the beam cracked, on which she knew the hunter had deceived her. The witch then tried to make good her escape but was hindered by the dogs, who clung to her clothes as long as they could. She escaped eventually and fled across the hills.

When the hunter arrived home he was told by his wife that the news in the district was that the Good Wife of Laggan lay very ill. He went to see her and when he uncovered the wounds on the witch's face she shrieked and died. That same night two travellers met a blood-stained woman running in the direction of a churchyard with two black dogs chasing her. They next met a black man on a black horse, who asked them if they had seen a woman being chased by dogs. When they said they had, he then asked them if she could be caught in the holy ground of the churchyard before the dogs caught her. They replied that they thought she might. A little later they were overtaken by the horseman returning with the woman lying on the horse's back in front of him, with the dogs' teeth fixed in her body. And that was the terrible end of the great witch of Laggan.

It was a witch who burnt all the ancient woodlands which once covered Inverness-shire and Ross-shire. These woods provided such a plentiful supply of timber that there was little demand for the Norway variety. This created an exporting problem for the King of Norway, who eventually decided to solve it by burning the Scottish woods. This, however, could be done only by some person skilled in the Black Arts. So he sent his daughter, Dona, to a school where all kinds of sorcery, magic and witchcraft were taught. On completing her education, she crossed to Scotland accompanied by her father and was sent ashore with a firebrand. Flying through the air, she rained fire down on the woodlands and caused much devastation. The Scots tried to take retaliatory action. But every time they approached her when she rested on the ground, she would rise from the earth and hide herself in a magic mist and evade the many attempts made to stop her journey of devastation. Eventually a wise man from Lochbroom hit on a plan. He gathered together a large herd of cattle, sheep and horses. Then, when Dona the witch was seen flying overhead he caused all the young animals to be separated from their mothers. This caused a great commotion, so loud in fact that it confused Dona and she began to sink to earth. A skilled archer was able to send an arrow through her heart and she fell to the ground, to wreak no more havoc on the Highland forests. Another version of this tale has it that while flying over Badenoch a man from the district saw her in the air and blessed her in the name of the Trinity. She at once crashed to the ground and was killed.

One day a Highland laird found himself seriously ill from some malady which his doctor could not diagnose. A skilful witch was consulted, who reported that it was a case of *corp creadh*—a clay image—and if the laird's life was to be saved the image must be destroyed. For this purpose it was necessary to obtain a person in possession of a *cnuimh-luirg*, a tracking bone. Such a person was found in the district who, with a bit of searching, discovered that the image was in a certain stream. The stream was searched and the image recovered. Within a week or two the laird was back to his former health. The people who had planned his death later left the district and never returned.

The following is a story of how six witches were got rid of from a district in Inverness-shire. All six of them were seen one evening making for a mill, with the obvious intention of stealing meal. On the way to the mill they had to cross a narrow wooden bridge which spanned a deep ravine. They were seen by several youths who at once decided to pit their wits against the witches and destroy them. They first took a number of planks from the middle of the bridge and then set fire to whin bushes near their cottages. The witches saw the fire from the mill, thought it was their homes ablaze and made their way back at top speed. The night, however, was dark and, not seeing that the bridge had been tampered with, all dropped into the deep waters below. Since that time no witch has dared to live in the district.

At Borgie, in the north of Sutherland, there lived a man called Matheson who had a ring made of pure gold and set with precious stones. The ring gave him the power of detecting witches and of healing any man or animal that suffered from their attentions. This 'Man of the Ring' became far-famed and many bewitched persons sought his services. Naturally every witch resented him and matters came to a head when a general meeting of witches was called to decide how to get rid of Matheson.

First they tried all their rites and incantations, to no avail. They then went in force to his house at Borgie with the intention to compel him to surrender the ring. But Matheson was aware of their plan and fled into the hills towards Strathnaver. The witches followed hard on his heels. He was being hard pressed by the hags when he met a woman who asked him the cause of his terror. He explained, pointing to the evil cloud of witches gaining on him, but felt he could trust the stranger. She told him to place the ring under a large boulder nearby, which he did; she then walked round it three times and it disappeared. When the witches caught up with him they demanded the ring; he told them it was under the stone which was out of sight for only a short time. They all waited and the stone appeared at which the hags, seeing that they were faced with a power they did not possess, fled the field and left Matheson alone. A cup and ring marked stone in the area is pointed out as being the stone in question. Tradition has it that if any bewitched persons were to go round it three times, repeating a certain incantation, they also would receive a wonderful power over witches.

Many times witches were called on to help sailors by giving them a favourable wind. There is the story of a Stornoway witch who was reputed to have the power to do this. A mariner, having been delayed at the port for some days through lack of wind, consulted her, paid the necessary price and received from her a string with three knots in it. When the first knot was undone he would get a favourable wind which would carry him nearly home, and then he was to undo the second. This he did and when within a mile of his home port he undid knot number two, whereupon there was a strong fresh breeze. As he entered the harbour, he thought there would be no harm in untying the third knot. So out of curiosity he undid the knot; no sooner had he done so than a hurricane blew up and his ship was cast high and dry on to an adjacent beach.

Another witch was consulted by a fisherman who had no luck. He crossed her hand with silver and for this she gave him a three-penny piece with the letters G.L. impressed on it. She told him to fix the coin to a rope which bound his nets. She said the letters stood for 'Good Luck'. Certainly, after that encounter the fisherman never had cause to complain about his luck.

That witches were not always waging war against the Highland community is told in another story about the three Lewis cats. At Torridon, in Wester Ross, there lived a man and his sister in a small house. One evening, before going out to do the milking, the sister put a large salmon on the fire to cook and told her brother that when the salmon was ready he was to take off the fish and put on a potful of potatoes. As he was watching the salmon three cats entered the house, one of which was red and blind in one eye. Taken with pity for the animals he welcomed them in and, boning the salmon, he threw them tidbits which they ate with obvious pleasure. After being fed, the cats left the house and disappeared into the waters of the nearby loch. Some time after that there was a very good herring fishing off Loch Roag, on the west coast of Lewis. Among those who cast their nets to reap the rich sea-harvest was the man from Torridon. After he had shot his nets he went ashore to look for lodgings. The first house he came to he entered and found himself welcomed by three women, who said they would be glad to repay his previous kindness. In astonishment the man asked where they had seen him before and he was reminded of the occasion when he fed three cats in his own home. The witches then told him that that particular day had been a memorable one for them. They went to Torridon to chase herring into the nets of their friends fishing there and had assumed the form of whales. When they got tired they landed on shore in the form of cats.

There is humour, too, in many of the stories about Highland witches. In a remote district of Argyll, a man, benighted, made for a small cottage and, as was the accepted custom, walked in to claim a night's hospitality. The old woman in the house, who seemed to be the only occupant, said that she could not put him up and asked him to leave. But he refused. Shortly after that, the old woman was joined by another who also asked him to leave; he replied he would not. A third woman appeared with the same request. But the man said he would not leave till daybreak. The three old women then sat round the fire and talked among themselves in low tones. The man, drowsy by now, watched them out of the corner of his eye. Then, half-asleep, he saw them dress as for a journey. The first woman put on a white cap or mulch and said "Off to London". To the man's surprise she sailed up through the smoke-hole in the roof. The second woman did the same and the third was about to put on her mulch when he ran over and snatched the cap out of her hand. "Off to London", said he, and in no time at all he found himself flying through the air. Half an hour later he found himself in the company of the other two women in a wine cellar in London. The three of them then sat down to enjoy the evening. Near dawn, the two ladies put on their mulches and said "Off to Argyll", whereupon they promptly disappeared. The man, eager to be away, fumbled but could not find his cap. Shrugging his shoulders he fell asleep, to be wakened rudely by the owner of the vaults who accused him of stealing wine without any intention to pay. He was also accused of being the thief who had, for some months previously, been depleting the cellars. In time the man was tried and condemned to die by hanging. The fatal day arrived and on the scaffold the poor man prepared to meet his fate. He put his hand in a pocket and what he thought to be a kerchief to wipe the sweat of fear from his brow, he found to be none other than the misplaced mulch. He turned to the hangman and asked if he could die with the white cap on his head. The request of a dying man, never to be refused, was granted. No sooner had he put the cap on his head when he said "Off to Argyll". At once he rose into the air and to the "great admiration" of the London crowd, disappeared from sight, with the scaffold. Soon afterwards he landed in his native country and with the wood of the scaffold built himself a cottage where he lived for many years. But never again did he don the cap and say "Off to London".

CHAPTER 2

The Evil Eye

ACCORDING TO HIGHLAND BELIEF the 'evil eye' is one which is animated by a discontented and unhappy mind, full of envy (*farmad*), covetousness (*sanntachadh*), and similar feelings which it conveys to objects it sees, to injure them in the process. The objects can include an animal, a person, or a possession of another. The belief in this gift of dubious value, which was sometimes associated with witchcraft, is universal and not particularly confined to the Scottish Highlands and Islands. However, the gift has been subjected to more investigation within the region than in any other, with the result that documentary evidence is available for scrutiny; though the investigations were usually carried out in the context of 'superstition' rather than in a more rational light seeking to understand and not to ridicule.

A number of Gaelic proverbs bring out the peculiar characteristic of the evil eye: "Fluich do shuil ma lean e rithe. " (Wet your eye lest it sticks to it—this is said by the owner when a person admires or covets an object; that is in case the viewer has the evil eye and the object becomes his or else dwindles away.) "The eye of the envious will split the stone." "Thuit droch shuil air." (An evil eye fell on him.) "Ghabh an droch shuil e." (The evil eye took him.) "Laidh droch shuil air." (An evil eye settled on him.) "Bhuail droch shuil e." (An evil eye struck him.) The very fact that the proverbs are widespread and laid claim to recent currency indicates that the belief in the evil eye was one of the harsh sides to life and living, in that nothing was sacred and outwith the influence of any controller, known or unknown, to gain some measure of control over. The proverbs indicate, too, the possible reasons for melancholy in a person by attributing to the evil eye the cause for a character change in that person.

The gift, such as it is, exists in both men and women, in friend and foe, and therefore its known presence created much fear in those who were potential recipients of the evil eye's nature. In some cases, particularly where animals were involved, the evil eye falling on them caused their subsequent death from some disease or misfortune. The main bright feature of the general darkness inherent in the possession of the evil eye was that in many cases it was possible to avert its influence, and to destroy its effect on an object, mainly by the use of charms. Highland folklore is full of stories telling of the effects of the influence and the many attempts to divert an object from the eye's attention. Whether many of the charms and ritual used to avert the influence relied on breaking the eye's natural force, or tended to strengthen the field or life force of an animate object remains to be seen. One must assume, however, that the nature of the evil eye was once understood and was able to be countered; the dilution of belief and understanding over many generations could well produce a debased set of rules and ritual to avert the influence, leading to the description of superstition by those to whom the evil eye was yet another manifestation of gullibility in rural people.

To those who investigated the evil eye less than a century ago, the influence was indeed accepted as another aspect of superstition, developed over many centuries as a part of an interesting folk culture. However, there may be now some grounds for suggesting that the gift has a factual basis; it may indeed be akin in its nature to autosuggestion and to the implanting of suggestions of physical default in another person. In the case of inanimate objects, the basis of the influence may well be founded in telekinesis or psychokinesis. This attribute is apparent in some humans and has attracted increasing attention in the past decade or so. Briefly, the possessor of the gift is able to interrupt mechanical devices so that their regularity of operation is disturbed, or objects are moved. Physical motion produced by the mind, and the ability to move things from a distance, are phenomena which have been subjected to scientific observation with the result that, in so far as any paranormal experience can be scientifically investigated, psychokinesis and telekinesis are now accepted as fact, simply because scientists find difficulty in working out the laws which seem to defy certain of the well-established physical laws which present-day science uses as its inviolate foundation.

It is left, then, to suggest that certain persons may well be able, either consciously for personal achievement of selfish purposes, or unconsciously, to transmit 'vibrations' (for want of a better word) to another person or an object and influence the life-force field of these to cause some default or damage. There may be an element of hypnotism in the influence of the evil eye, coupled with telepathy, in the case of people who discover that they have fallen ill from some disease or physical malfunction, picked up from an unknown source. In the case of animals, there may be ability in the possessor of the 'eye' to home in on the health wavelength of a beast and implant in the beast's life-force field a syncopation which causes damage to the beast, resulting in illness and death. If it is on record that a human being can produce telekinetic effects from a distance, then the influence of the 'eye' might well cause objects to lose their character, for example (and this is a favourite instance in Highland lore) the loss of the substance or goodness in milk or cheese. It could be that much of what has been attributed to 'superstition' is in fact based on the real essence of folklore: the knowledge that the human mind can operate on planes inaccessible at the present time to many, but still accessible to some who become popular 'marvels', such as Uri Geller and Edward Marshall, who perform with ease tasks which are far beyond the ability of the normal person. The fact that Mrs Nelya Mikhailova in Russia can separate the white of an egg from the yolk, and move the two apart from a distance of two metres under the tightest experimental controls, indicates that the power of the evil eye may well be more than a facet of superstition. Whatever its basis, it is obvious, as with other aspects of 'superstition' and folklore, that there remain many domains of human experience which bear close investigation to yield the possibility of enlarging the area of operation over which human life and living can range.

Much of the evidence for the existence of the evil eye in the Highlands and Islands is located in the corpus of knowledge popularly categorised as 'folklore' end is embodied in the extended work on the subject by Dr R. C. MacLagan, in his *Evil Eye in the Western Highlands*, published in 1902. In an interesting chapter entitled 'Science versus Eolas', MacLagan indicates that the receipt of the evil eye was a disaster which no medical man could prevent from proceeding to its inevitable course; but it was also something which a person, well-versed in the right kind of knowledge (eolas) for its cure, could reverse its effects to achieve success.

MacLagan took his belief, or willingness to believe, in the evil eye only so far as could be supported by his theory that the 'eye' was a natural fear instilled in those whose possessions became the object of admiration on the part of another; the natural irritation felt at the hostile look of a neighbour; the unease felt when a stranger passes a remark on the health of a beast or the beauty of a child; and the possible insincerity of one's fellows. He places the evil eye fairly and squarely in the realm of superstition:

> Selfishness, natural to all of us, is apt to find expression in our habits, however much we may disguise it by religious or charitable profession. Were it a part of our nature to have for our neighbour the same affection we have for ourselves, no such superstition as that of the Evil Eye could have arisen . . . Right or wrong, the theory here advanced accounts, satisfactorily, as far as the writer can judge, for the present-day widespread belief in Scotland of the power for evil of the glance of the human eye.

But for all his disbelief in the 'eye as a force for evil, MacLagan pressed forward his investigations and his book is a monument of that work. Had he been able to lean on present-day knowledge he might have shifted his stance to include a small element of belief in the evil eye. His investigations, for all that they were conducted from a disbeliever's viewpoint, were thorough; indeed, this present chapter owes as much to him as to others who, travelling along the byways of Highland folklore, have recorded instances of the evil eye as they met them.

As usual, Gaelic, the language of the region for commonalty and intellectuals alike, is a source of information about the nature of the evil eye. The eye always causes the *toradh* of cattle and milk to diminish. This word means fruit or produce, and its use implies that the influence of the eye took the essence of goodness from a product; the more natural or organic the product, such as an animal, milk or cheese, the more effective was the influence of the eye. An object under the influence was said to be *air-an-cronachadh*, or harmed or otherwise hurt. Many of those whom MacLagan interviewed indicated that while *buidseachas* (witchcraft) had disappeared from their district, the evil eye remained to cause distress and consternation within the community. Even today in some parts of the region the belief in its existence persists, though to a lesser extent than two decades ago when a ceremony in the Hebrides was witnessed in connection with the averting of the influence.

Cron means a fault or defect and the verb used is an expression of an opinion that something is wrong with an object.

Although it was believed that anyone might have the evil eye, and have this gift without being aware of it themselves, certain persons were suspected of it by their appearance. The eye was a common attribute of older women in a community, perhaps an echo of the witchcraft days when a witch could only be an elderly person; men, too, had the gift but they figure less frequently in stories about the eye's influence and achievements. Persons with eyes of a different colour were immediately suspect, as well they might with their pale eye coming to rest on a favourite possession. However, parti-coloured eyes account for less than a tenth of the cases of ill ascribed to the evil eye.

Many of the instances of the eye are concerned with injury or death to animals, these being particularly susceptible to its influence. One woman of Heynish, Tiree, would not allow her husband to look at his own fold of cattle for, whenever he did so, one of the best cows would be found dead the following day. Last century a farmer near Campbeltown was visited one year by drovers who wanted to view a fine beast with which he always refused to part. The drovers admired the cow at great length and made some good offers for the animal, all of which were refused. After much argument the drovers left, feeling rather disgruntled at the waste of their time. But no sooner than they had done so than the animal began to walk about in complete circles; despite efforts, the animal could not be got out of her perambulations and had to be killed. It was believed that one of the drovers had put the evil eye influence on the beast.

From the many hundreds of instances of evil eye, or what has been thought to be the result of the affliction, one can only make some kind of representative selection to indicate the wide area of human interests and activities over which the 'eye' could range. Of the means available to avert the influence, or to counteract it once it had struck, again a representative selection is given, based on those which are not so obvious as outright and rank superstition, but means which have themselves a para-factual basis (if one can be permitted to use such a term) as has, possibly, the influence of the evil eye.

A woman who lived on Loch Awe-side, who was believed to have the evil eye, and whose father was also credited with it, exchanged some brood hens with a neighbour. She brought her own hen and was going to take away the one to be exchanged. In the absence of the mistress, the girl who was keeping the house was going to give the cow a drink, and the woman accompanied her. There was nothing wrong with the cow at first, but later in the day the cow's calf died and the cow herself began to take some fits; though she lived for a while she never recovered. When night came the hens began to crow and next morning two of them were found dead. The hen that had been brought was then put on the eggs, but she escaped and was last seen in the nearby hills. All these events were the consequence of the evil eye.

Even more common than injury to cows and calves is the deterioration of milk. One woman told how she was churning butter one evening when the house was paid a visit by a young man from a neighbour's house. Just before the man entered the house the butter was ready for taking off and, to entertain him, the woman stopped and talked a while with him. After he left she went back to her churn to find the butter gone with only swelled milk, the consequence of the evil eye.

One man had a fine white horse which all admired who viewed it. One day a neighbour, who bore no ill-will to the owner, stood beside the horse and commented that it had good strong limbs. No sooner had he left than the horse fell to the ground and kicked as if in great pain. At first it was supposed to be an attack of colic. The owner thought otherwise and sent for a woman known to have skill with the evil eye. Her visit paid off for, using skills and charms, she cured the horse; the fact that she used no medical relief confirmed that the animal had indeed been afflicted by the influence.

The following is an instance from Tarbet (Ross-shire):

> One of my sisters was blighted by a woman who lived beside them. She was well known for her uncanny ways. The way the thing happened was this: The little girl was tied on an elder sister's back, and they were sent out for a walk. They had not gone far when the woman in question came forward and, putting the shawl back from the child's face, said, "What a pretty little girl! Which of them is this?" When the children returned from their walk their mother found that the little one was very ill; on questioning the elder girl she was told about the meeting with the old woman. On hearing this she sent for the woman and charged her with having hurt her child. The woman protested that she had not done the child any injury, but the elder girl spoke up and said, "Yes, you looked at her and said she was pretty, and did not bless her." The woman admitted this and said that if she had done any harm to the child she was sorry for it, but it could be sorted if wrong had been done. She then operated a charm and the sickly child was soon as brisk as ever.

A man from Campbeltown:

> I am sure I do not know about these things, for I have never seen anything of it myself, but I mind my neighbour over there saying to me one day not long ago that a woman was going past some time before that, and she began to praise one of his cows, saying what a grand udder she had and such fine teats. No doubt the cow was good, she said, and a fine milker; but after that day her milk went from her.

An instance from South Uist:

> There was a woman near her father's house believed to have a very bad eye, and to be able to do mischief with it. Her aunt was very careful as much as possible to keep out of this woman's sight, and if she happened to come about at churning time her aunt would put the churn so that the woman would not see it. She would not sell a pound of butter to her for any consideration. The curious thing was that although that woman could take away the produce from other people's cows, she seemed unable to make any profit of it for herself. It was just her envious and malicious nature that made her take it [the produce] from other people, although it was not going to benefit herself. She was well known by all the people in the district, and they all suspected her of the practice of witchcraft. It was on account of this suspicion that selling butter to her was objected to.

The following instance of the evil eye occurred in the island of Grimsay, North Uist, with a recorded date of February 1906. The record tells of a man from Benbecula who went to the island to buy a horse, an animal of a handsome and showy breed for which a price could be asked in excess of what he could really afford. The horse belonged to a man named MacAulay, residing on a croft at Mas-Ghrimsa. The buyer obtained local reports about the animal and set his heart on it. The next day, as he made his way through the island, he passed MacAulay's croft, greeted the crofter and said a word or two in praise of the animal. That evening the horse became very ill. MacAulay tried all the remedies he could think of but to no avail. Gradually the thought of evil eye came to him and he sent off immediately for a local woman known to have powers which could counteract the evil eye. Her cure was the use of *Eolas-an-t-snathlain*, the charm of the thread.

MacAulay told her of his horse's illness and she set to work at once. She procured three pieces of woollen thread, red, blue and green, which she twined into a three-stranded thread, knotting them together. The complete thread she gave to MacAulay with instructions to tie it round the tail of the sick horse, on the bony stump under the long hair of the tail. This MacAulay did and the horse was cured within the hour.

The woman, a Mrs MacLean, used her fingers and teeth to twine the thread, during which she crooned a rune, which invoked the aid of Peter and Paul in a general blessing on her work. The cure on the horse was bruited abroad and Mrs MacLean found herself approached by a person interested in the matter. In an interview Mrs MacLean admitted that she had this power, among others, and that her mother had had it before her. During her cures she was not conscious of any 'possession', but simply carried out the process believing towards a successful conclusion and never accepting the possibility of defeat. She had never failed in any case brought to her attention. She also said that she could tell when the evil or illness had been caused by an evil or envious wish or was merely accidental. If the latter, then she had no difficulty as she had no opposition to overcome. If the former cause obtained, she felt the opposition to her curative efforts and had to stem and overcome the influences pitted against her. If the opposition was severe she emerged from the contest quite exhausted and on several occasions had to take to her bed for a day or two. Mrs MacLean said that on one occasion it took her four days to recover.

Mrs MacLean indicated that her gift could diminish if she failed to cultivate the 'Christian graces'; it would "wane and fade away and disappear". Mrs MacLean was known locally as a woman of integrity and purity of life. What her power was she did not know, but surmised that it was a natural development of a sense which was dormant in most people.

One interesting aspect of Mrs MacLean's gift can be compared with the present-day Mrs Nelya Mikhailova, mentioned earlier. This is the mention by Mrs MacLean that after a serious encounter with the strong influence of the evil eye she found herself in a state of exhaustion. It is on record that Mrs Mikhailova, after a test of mind over matter in which she separated the yolk of an egg from the white, she lost over two pounds in weight, in a period of thirty minutes, and was at the end of the day so weak that she had to take to her bed; she was also unable to sleep for several days. Russian scientists have developed instruments able to record and chart the life-force field of a human being; and neurophysiologists in Canada are using a field detector to determine at a distance whether a patient is in a state of anxiety or otherwise. Is there then an element of fact in the cures for evil eye involving people with special gifts? The visible trappings of thread and other items may well be mere vehicles for mind concentration, coupled with the use of words, to effect a reversal of the influence of the eye.

The belief in evil eye affecting cattle and other livestock still exists: Some thirty years ago in North Uist a veterinary surgeon was confronted with some strange instances while he made his rounds of stock in the island. One day he was called in by an old woman to examine her cow. The beast appeared to be in perfect health until a routine sample of her milk was drawn off. When the sample tube had been left standing for some time it was observed that all the fats had separated out to the bottom, leaving a clear liquid above a thick sediment. The sample was submitted to the laboratories in Edinburgh of the Department of Agriculture by whom the vet was informed that the milk appeared to be perfectly normal. More than puzzled, the vet informed the old woman who merely nodded her head in a knowing way. Some weeks later the cow was reported to be completely fit again and giving a normal yield—without the vet's intervention. He paid a visit to the croft and was startled to see the cow in a nearby field with a long plaited woollen cord tied to its tail. It transpired that the old lady, convinced that her cow had been bewitched, had gone for a charm to a "man in the north islands", who had a reputation for practising white magic. He gave her the cord which he had spun with his own hands and told her that the cow would be well again as soon as the cord was tied to its tail.

The making of a *snaithe* or charm of plaited wool of varying colours was common. The late Calum I. MacLean, of the School of Scottish Studies in Edinburgh, said in 1947 he saw an old woman spinning such a charm and chanting a spell as she worked. This was a rare privilege as the spell was usually kept a secret of great potency. This woman was well known throughout the Hebrides and her charms were often to be seen adorning even the radiator caps of lorries and tractors.

Another instance brings together two supernatural elements, second sight and the evil eye, from the same island. The same vet was called in to attend a horse belonging to a crofter from Carinish. When he arrived the animal was lying in the byre, clearly beyond all cure. The crofter and his neighbours immediately set about digging a grave while waiting for the horse to die (an example of the custom of leaving a dying beast to fight out its own battle with death). Across the road from the crofter lived an old woman who would have been in perfect health had she not for many years been confined to her bed with chronic rheumatism.

While the men were busy digging the horse's grave, one of them, with a reputation for having the second sight, observed coming towards the byre a man known to be possessed of the evil eye. Turning to his companions he said: "He with the evil eye will go into the byre and soon after the horse will be well again." The man, indeed, went into the byre in the company of the owner and a short while later the horse got up on its legs and made for the open fields, galloping across the machair seemingly little the worse for its experience.

While the assembled company looked in amazement at the miraculous cure, the man with second sight said: "He with the evil eye will now go over to the house of the old woman and it is not long after that she will be living." Even as he spoke the man with the 'eye' went into the old woman's house, to emerge shortly afterwards "with a grim look on his face" to announce to those gathered at the roadside that the old woman was dead. This is an unusual example, in the corpus of tales of the evil eye, of the apparent transmigration of death.

The store of cures for the evil eye amassed over the centuries contains much which is ritual; not a few contain elements of what might be regarded as faith-healing, particularly where humans are concerned. Inevitably mystery was a feature of many cures. One such was handed down in one family from male to female, from female to male, and was effective only when thus transmitted. Before it was pronounced over a particular case of sickness, the operator went to a stream, where the living and the dead pass alike, and took some water into a wooden ladle, in the name of the Holy Trinity. In no case is the ladle of metal. On returning a wife's gold ring, a piece of gold, of silver and of copper were put into the ladle. The sign of the cross was then made and a rhyme repeated in a slow recitative manner, the name of the person or animal under treatment being mentioned towards the end. In the case of an animal, a woollen thread, generally of the natural colour of the sheep, was tied round the tail. The consecrated water was then given as a draught and sprinkled over the head and backbone. In the case of a cow, the horns and the space between the horns were carefully anointed. The remainder of the water, no drop of which must have touched the ground previously, was poured over a corner-stone, threshold flag or other immovable stone or rock, which was said to split if the sickness was severe.

In the little village of Kiltarlity, Inverness-shire, lives Mrs Annie Fraser, a white witch who claims success in curing people of troubles both in this country and on the Continent of Europe. She says that her spell-lifting powers were inherited from her parents and grandparents. Before sunrise she gathers water from a burn close to the Bridge of the Living and the Dead. Into the pail she puts her wedding ring and a silver coin; over these she adds water from the burn, blessing it with these words: "I, Mrs Fraser, sprinkle this water on . . ." She mentions the person's name and continues: ". . . In the name of the Father, Son and Holy Spirit I bless you and may all evil depart from you." In explanation she says: "It is essential that the ritual be performed before sunrise and that there is gold and silver together in the water."

CHAPTER 3

Second Sight

OF ALL THE SUPERNATURAL characteristics of the Highlands and Islands, that of second sight is the most widely recognised and accepted by native and visitor alike who have, at the very least, a nodding acquaintance with the pronouncements of the great protagonist of the gift: Coinneach Odhar, or the Brahan Seer. He, however, is only one, albeit shadowy, figure, in a vivid gallery of tellers of the future, operators in an area of the occult which goes back for its origins into the mists of Highland times past, and yet is as lively and significant in Highland rural life today as it ever was. Many people tend to think that possession of second sight is a gift, in that the ability to foretell future events can be turned to some material advantage of some significance. Instead, this seemingly advantageous character of the gift never seems to materialise: the gift, if such it is, is more regarded as an affliction than something beneficial either to seer or those seen. The general view of the Highlander to second sight is that of the Church: that these 'things' do exist, though in some instances they may be due to delusion or some mental disorder which, somehow, enhances latent gifts of sight in a person not otherwise known to have the gift.

The Gaelic word for second sight is *da-shealladh*, which means 'two sights', perhaps conveying the idea that a vision of the world of sense is one sight, but a vision of another world, populated by people living, but not within the actual sight of the seer, or living but in another time, is another, rarer, sight. Through this faculty, seers can 'see' the dead returned to earth, revisiting the physical world for some purpose, and also see wraiths, fetches, doubles or apparitions of the living, either in the present time or in a future time. Visions seem to fall into two general categories: those which involve living people, contemporary with the seer and often his or her own close friends or relations, who appear as wraiths and might be taken as 'precognition'—the ability to foretell events about to happen, and which do occur within a short time of the forecast; the other category contains visions of events which often involve those not yet born and which are more difficult both to explain in contemporary language, images and meanings, and also to establish their time. The latter sights are contained in the visions of the true seer: the person able to project far into the future and, though he or she has no means of knowing whether the vision will come to pass, are sufficiently convinced of their gift that the details of it are set down and recorded.

Sights involving the contemporary living also take in what is known as *déjà vu*, the ability of many people to sense that their immediate experience is one that has already occurred. The time gap between the *déjà vu* experience and its actual occurrence is small and can often be in seconds. This sense of experiencing the past in the present is one aspect of the seer's gift.

The object seen by the seer, the phantasm, is called in Gaelic *taibhs* (pronounced 'taish'), the person seeing it *taibhsear*, and the gift of vision, in addition to its name of second sight, is *taibhsearachd*. A number of words in Gaelic referring to spirits and ghosts begin with the syllable 'ta', as in:

> *Tannas*, or *tannasg*—This is a spectre, generally of the dead, with the associated idea of a more shadowy, unsubstantial and spiritual being than a *bochdan*.

> *Tamhasg*—The shade or double of a living person; this is the common name for apparitions by which men are haunted and with which, according to the doctrine of second sight, they have to hold assignations.

> *Tachar*—This is a rare and now almost obsolete word; its derivatives, however, *tacharan* and *tachradh*, are still in common use. The words are often associated with places, such as Sron an Tachair, the Ghost-Haunted Nose (a rock between Kinloch Rannoch and Druin-a-Chaisteal in Perthshire) where faint mysterious noises are said to be heard and on passing which the solitary wayfarer is accosted by a mysterious spirit which joins him in the hollow below. In Iona there is Imire Tachair, a ridge leading from the ecclesiastical buildings to the hill, which, until the moor through which it runs was drained, formed an elevation above a sheet of water, a likely place to be haunted. The derivatives *tachradh* and *tacharan* are applied to a small and helpless person.

> *Taslaich*—This is a supernatural premonition, felt or heard, but not seen. The word is also applied to ghosts of living persons, as in the saying "Taslaich nan daoine beo", the ghosts of the living, usually associated with premonitions of funerals.

> *Taradh*—These are noises (*straighlich*) heard at night through the house, indicating a change of tenants, pointing to a premonition, evidenced by mysterious sounds, of a coming event.

Taran—This is the ghost of an unbaptised child, not now used as a common word in Gaelic.

Tasg—This is perhaps a contraction of *tamhasg*, used in the phrase "Eigheach taisg", the cry or wail of a fetch.

Taghairm—This is the spirit-call, noises like calling voices which people often hear, but which have no traceable source or origin.

The origin of wraiths of the living is based on the supposition that people have a counterpart, or other self, an alter ego, which goes about unbeknown to themselves, with their exact same voices, features, form and dress, and is visible only to those who have second sight. This wraith is sometimes termed by mediums the 'aura', which often becomes strong in texture in times of personal stress or crisis, to the extent that some people claim to "come out of themselves". It was commonly held that the wraith was independent of all thought and volition on the part of those whom it represented, as well as on the part of the seer himself. It was part of the belief that if the person whose double was seen was spoken to and told to cease his persecutions or hauntings, the annoyance came to an end. However, that person was usually utterly unaware of the fact that his alter ego was the cause of other people's distress.

It was often given to a seer to interpret the fate of the person whose wraith was being observed. If the apparition was in bedclothes, a death was foretold; if it was in everyday clothes, the death was not imminent but in the near future. However, some grave-cloths were supposed to indicate good fortune (*ion-aodach aigh*) while others indicated death (*lion-aodach bais*) and it needed a skilful seer to distinguish between them. If the person was to be drowned at sea, phosphorescent gleams (*teine-sionnachain*), such as are commonly seen on Hebridean seas on summer nights, appeared round the figure, or else the clothes seemed to drip with water. This latter was a common apparition to the writer's grandmother, who often received a constant stream of worried relatives of fishermen at sea, whose boats were long overdue. Visions were not always associated with melancholy events, deaths, impending funerals or disasters. Often visions were beheld of happy events such as forthcoming marriages.

As already mentioned, the gift of second sight was not looked upon as something to be envied or desired. Frequently seers wished they had no such gift, but often, perhaps because it ran in the family, they were dogged with it. Other seers found their gift in the form of an advanced faculty early in life, while others became aware of it in later life. Sometimes it was said to be the result of hereditary disease, malformation or weakness in the visual organs, and derangements in both

47

mental and bodily health. The gift was not voluntarily controlled; rather it came and went without the option of the seer. People known to have the gift were credited with a peculiar look about the eyes. One man in Harris for instance was described as "always looking up and never looking at you straight in the face". The seers tended to be of a brooding and melancholy disposition and were thus obvious to their fellows.

Martin Martin, the 'gent' from Skye, describes seers and their visions in his book on the Western Islands of Scotland which was first published in 1703. The Swiss scientist, Necker de Saussure, and that indefatigable tourist, Thomas Pennant, both mention one of the famous instances of second sight: Lord President Forbes foretelling, at the time of the Battle of Prestonpans (1745), that the Jacobite Rising would end at Culloden (April 1746).

Martin Martin defined second sight as

> a singular Faculty of Seeing an otherwise invisible Object, without any previous Means us'd by the Person that sees it for that end; the Vision makes such a lively impression upon the Seers, that they neither see nor think of any thing else, except the Vision, as long as it continues: and then they appear pensive or jovial, according to the Object which was represented to them.

He quotes some thirty cases, most of them of Skye origin, and an account of the significance of the signs as perceived by seers. Martin, who was antagonistic towards all superstitions which offended his religious convictions, was, however, firmly convinced of the existence of second sight and went some way to answer the objections of sceptics to the existence of such a faculty. From Martin's time there grew an interest in second sight, to be developed by Samuel Pepys, the Revd Robert Kirk of Aberfoyle, John Aubrey, Dr Samuel Johnson, and Sir Walter Scott and Kirkpatrick Sharpe, though the main interest of the latter was in witchcraft.

The subject received something of a final accolade in 1894 when, as reported by the *Oban Times*: "We understand that several members of the Society for Psychical Research are at present on a tour of the West Highlands and Islands collecting information from the natives in regard to that peculiar faculty said to be possessed by many people, especially in the Highlands, and popularly known as 'second sight', as well as kindred subjects." The Society circulated some 2,000 potential individuals in the region whom they thought might offer some information on the occurrence, belief, current prevalence and practice of the gift. The response to the Society's questionnaire was very poor and occasioned the thought that face-to-face encounters would be a better tactic to use to yield the necessary data on the subject. In the event, this proved to be more successful and it uncovered a number of persons, including Fr Allan MacDonald, parish priest of Eriskay, all of whom had much to say and report on second sight. In addition, a lot of indirect evidence was obtained. The main stumbling block, however, was the simple fact that many extant seers were monoglot Gaelic speakers and were therefore inaccessible to the questions of the equally monoglot English-speaking members of the Society's research team. Perhaps the most valuable vein of information obtained by the Society was that previously mined by Fr Allan MacDonald. He had, by dint of hard work in gaining the confidence of his parishioners, garnered a rich harvest of tales, anecdotes, Gaelic words and stories, many of which included instances of second sight. Despite the possibilities which existed in the region accessible to native Gaelic speakers, had they been invited to join the team, the Society eventually failed to produce the promised, and eagerly awaited, reports of the results of the Second Sight Enquiry in the Highlands. Even so, the Society deserved credit for recognising, in its role and status of a learned body, that there existed interesting facets of Highland oral culture, however folk-based, and that this was worthy of serious investigation.

The corpus of literature about Highland second sight is large and extensive in range, and includes instances which show up the application and function of the gift in many aspects of life affecting both the individual and his community; the instances also take in the short-term foretelling of events to happen within hours, days, weeks or a few months of the prognostication, and long-term projections into the future, involving decades and centuries, such as are characteristic of many of the visions credited to Coinneach Odhar, the Brahan Seer.

Among the earliest recorded instances is that quoted by Martin Martin, who heard of the vision fully eighteen months before the event took place. The vision concerned a seer in the island of Eigg "who frequently saw an apparition of a man in a red coat lined with blue, and having on his head a strange sort of blue cap with a very high cock on the fore part of it, and that the man who there appeared was kissing a comely maid in the village werein the seer dwelt." About a year and a half later, a Major Ferguson landed on the island with 600 men to reduce the islanders who had been 'out' for King James. The soldiers wreaked their vengeance on the islanders. Other prophecies involved the sight of red-coat soldiers long before they made their appearance in the Highlands to cover the moors with their scourging activities. The Revd John Frazer, Minister of Tiree and Coll, and Dean of the Isles, wrote about second sight in 1707, and quoted the following instances of the phenomenon on Tiree and other of the islands of the Inner Hebrides.

The first instance is by a servant of my own, who had the trust of my barn, and nightly lay in the same. One day he told me he would not any longer lye there, because nightly he had seen a dead corpse in his winding sheet straightened beside him, particularly at the south side of the barn. About an half-year thereafter a young man, that had formerly been my servant, dangerously sick and expecting death, would needs be carried near my house, and shortly thereafter he died, and was laid up a night before he was buried in the same individual barn and place that was foretold, and immediately the servant that foretold this and came to me and minded me of the prediction, which was clearly out of my mind until he spoke of it.

The second instance is after this manner. I was resolved to pay a visit to an English gentleman, Sir William Sacheverill, who had a commission from the English Court of Admiralty to give his best tryall to find out gold or money or any other thing of note in one of the ships of the Spanish Armada that was blown up in the Bay of Topper-Mory, in the Sound of Mull. And having condescended upon the number of men that were to go with me, one of the number was a handsome boy that waited upon my own person, and, about an hour before I made sail, a woman, that was also one of my own servants, spoke to one of the seamen and bade him dissuade me to take that boy along with me, or, if I did, I should not bring him back alive. The seaman answered he had not confidence to tell me such unwarrantable trifles. I took my voyage and sailed the length of Topper-Mory, and having stayed two or three nights with a Literat and Ingenious Gentleman, who himself had collected many observations of the Second-Sight in the Isle of Man, and compared his notes and mine together, in the end I took leave of him. In the meantime my boy grew sick of a vehement bloody flux, the winds turned so cross that I could neither sail nor row. The boy died with me the eleventh night from his decumbiture, and the seaman to whom the matter was foretold related the whole story when he saw it verified. I carried the boy's corpse aboard with me, and after my arrival and his burial I called suddenly for the woman and asked her at what warrand she had to foretell the boy's death. She said that she had no other warrand but that she saw the boy walking with me in the fields, sewed up in his winding sheets from top to toe, and that she had never seen this in others but that she found that they shortly thereafter died, and therefore concluded that he would die too, and that shortly.

The third instance was thus: Duncan Campbell, brother-gentle-man to Archibald Campbell of Invere, a gentleman of singular piety and considerable knowledge, especially in Divinity, told me a strange thing of himself; that he was at a time in Kintyre, having then some employment there, and one morning walking in the fields he saw a dozen men carrying a bier and knew them all but one, and when he looked again all was vanished. The very next day the same company came the same way carrying a bier, and he going to meet them found that they were but eleven in number, and that himself was the twelfth, though he did not notice it before, and it is to be observed that this gentleman never saw anything of this kind before or after, till his dying day. Moreover that he was of such solid judgment and devote conservation that his report deserves an unquestionable credit.

Frazer tried to probe into the phenomenon, explaining it in the context of the ideas of his day, in terms of species or images coming from things, passing into the brain through eye and ear, and there stored up in order in its various compartments. He accounts for visions —sounds being seen and heard—on the principle of the present-day recording by electronic means which allows for playback of sound and vision by video-tape, the brain being the facility for the 'replay'. This solution is possibly near the mark, in that it takes in the idea of time-warping, allowing future events to appear as contemporary happenings. When Frazer came to sticky patches he referred the matter as an example of the direct will of God, since he was satisfied that the visions were sent for the edification of believers.

In 1763 a small octavo volume was published in Edinburgh on behalf of 'Theophilus Insulanus', believed to be a Minister on Skye by the name of Macpherson. He had, it seemed, travelled extensively throughout the Highlands and Islands and uncovered much which so impressed him that he entitled his book *A Treatise on the Second Sight, Dreams and Apparitions, with several instances sufficiently attested; and an appendix of others equally authentic.* The author accounted for the gift on natural grounds, being convinced, through the many instances of prophecies and visions he cited, that the gift was based on certain physical and mental disturbances. He was careful to point out that the seers were possessors of "minds of a melancholy cast" and "in some instances they are weak-sighted". His theory aligns itself with that which supposed genius to be the product of disease. His examples are stories which were, according to him, given on the authority of the narrators: "persons of undoubted veracity who had no interest or design to falsify or disguise the truth of their narrations".

Donald Mackinnon, an "honest tenant" in Halistra, in Waternish, relates that in the harvest of 1760, in the dusk of the evening, as he was binding and putting together the corn, on a sudden he saw a neighbour of his, followed by a throng of people carrying a corpse, go right through a field of standing corn belonging to himself. Naturally he was not pleased. However, through fear that it might be a vision, he

51

did not choose to challenge his neighbour. His wife and family held that the vision would soon be verified. He went out in the early morning, found the corn standing, and was satisfied that it was a vision. About a year after he saw his neighbour and a company with corpse in reality coming through the same field from Greshernish, to bury it at the church-yard of Trumpan.

Christina Macaskill told Macpherson that she often had the second-sight, but not with any satisfaction.

Her first experience of it was, when on one occasion she sat by the fireside, she saw one Kenneth Macaskill, who lived at some distance from her house, taking a sheep belonging to herself and cutting its throat. She immediately rose and went to the mane's house, forced the door open, and there and then found the man in the very act which she foresaw in the vision. She identified the sheep by "Challenging her mark on it". The thief, finding he was caught, gave her three or four ells of new linen, which he said was price enough for her sheep, and then strongly recommended to keep the whole thing a secret.

Angus Campbell was a tacksman in Ensay, in Harris, when he saw a fleet of nine ships coming under sail to a place called Corminish, opposite to his house, where they dropped anchor. Both he and his family, including his servant, he avers, took particular notice of the large sloop among the ships. As the place where they moored was not a safe harbour, he sent word to others of his servants to come that they might send a boat to pilot these ships to a safer anchorage. On their coming up to him, and while deliberating what to do, the scene gradually disappeared. This may have been an optical delusion, but the remarkable thing is added that two years thereafter the same number of ships, including the remarkable sloop, came and dropt anchor at Corminish. The story is vouched by many living witnesses, he says, including the Rev. Mr Kenneth Macaulay, the minister of Harris.

Donald MacLeod was one of the MacLeods of Lewis, who claim descent from the Kings of Norway, who once ruled over the whole of the Hebrides and the Isle of Man. He told Theophilus that a certain young girl was contracted to a gentleman in Lewis equal to her in birth and other circumstances. A Seer, who lived in the family, frequently told the young lady that she would never be married to that man. Even when the parson came to join their hands, the bride and bridegroom being completely dressed and ready waiting to fulfil the ceremony, the Seer persisted in what he had so often asserted. In the meantime, the bride having stepped out of the room after night fell, she was met by a gentleman at the head of twelve persons, who carried her to a boat nearby, and conducting her to an island at some distance from the mainland, waited there until they were married, and the Seer's prediction fulfilled.

John Aubrey, a Fellow of the Royal Society at Gresham College in London, was interested in the subject from a distance. He obtained his information from a correspondent, "a Learned Friend of Mine in Scotland", and published the substance of letters in the *Miscellanies*, printed in 1696. Aubrey first drew up some questions to be answered and received replies which were to his great satisfaction and impressed him so much that the instances he cited were "nothing but the verity".

Query 4—If these events, which Second-sighted men discover, or fore-tell, be visibly represented to them, and acted as it were, before their eyes? Answer—Affirmatively, they see these things visibly, but none sees them but themselves; for instance, if a man's fatal end be hanging, they'll see a gibbet, or a rope about his neck; if beheaded, they'll see the man without a head; if drowned, they'll see water up to his throat; if unexpected death, they'll see a winding-sheet about his head; all of which are presented to their view. One instance I had from a gentleman here, of a Highland gentleman of the Mackdonalds' who having a brother that came to visit him, saw him coming in wanting a head; yet told not his brother he saw any such thing; but within 24 hours thereafter his brother was taken (being a murderer) and his head cut off and sent to Edinburgh. Many such instances might be given.

I cannot pass by an instance I have from a very honest man in the next parish, who told me it himself. That his wife, being big with child, near her delivery, he buys half a dozen boards to make her a bed 'gainst the time she lay in. The boards lying at the door of his house, there comes an old fisherwoman, yet alive, and asked him whose were those boards? He told her they were his own. She asked again for what use he had them? He replied, for a bed. She again said—Intend them for what use you please, she saw a dead corpse lying on them, and that they would be a coffin; which struck the honest man to his heart, fearing the death of his wife. But when the old woman went off, he calls presently for the carpenter to make the bed, which was accordingly done, but shortly after the honest man had a child died. whose coffin was made of the ends of those boards.

In the meantime I shall tell you what I have had from one of the Masters of our College here (a North-countryman both by birth and education, in his younger years), who made a journey in the harvest time into the shire of Ross, and, at my desire, made some enquiry there concerning the Second-Sight. He reports that there they told him many instances of this knowledge which he had forgotten, except two. The first, one of his sisters, a young gentlewoman, staying with a friend at some 30 miles distance from her father's home, and the ordinary place of her residence. One who had the Second-Sight in the family where she was, saw a young man attending her as she went up and down the house, and this was about three months before her marriage. The second is of a woman in that country who is reputed to have the Second-Sight and declared, that eight days before the death of a gentleman there she saw a bier, or coffin cover with a cloth which she knew, carried as it were to the place of burial, and attended with a great company, one of which told her it was the corpse of such a person, naming that gentleman, who died eight days after.

Those that have this faculty of the Second-Sight see only things to come, which are to happen shortly thereafter, and sometimes foretell things which fall out three or four years after. For instance, one told his master that he saw an arrow in such a man through his body, and yet no blood came out, and if that came not to pass he would be deemed an impostor. But about 5 or 6 years after the man died and being brought to his burial-place, there arose a debate anent his grave, and it came to such a height that they drew arms and bended their bows, and one letting off an arrow shot through the dead body on the bier-trees, and so no blood could issue out of a dead man's wound. Thus his sight could not inform him whether the arrow should be shot in him alive or dead, neither could he condescend whether near or far off.

Aubrey's *Miscellanies* also contain a "copy of a letter written to myself by a gentleman's son in Strathspey, being a student in Divinity, concerning the Second-Sight". In this letter several instances are given —"only those attested by several of good credit yet alive":

And first, Andrew Mackpherson of Clunie in Badenoch, being in sute of Laird of Gareloch's daughter, as he was upon a day going to Gareloch, the Lady Gareloch was going somewhere from her house within Kenning to the very road which Clunie was coming.

The Lady perceiving him said to her attendants that yonder was Clunie going to see his mistress. One that had this Second-Sight in her company replied and said—"If yon be he, unless he marry within six months he'll never marry". The Lady asked how did he know that? He said very well; for I see him, saith he, all inclosed in his winding-sheet, except his nostrils and his mouth, which will also close up within six months. Which happened even as he foretold; within the said space he died, and his brother, Duncan Macpherson, this present Clunie, succeeded.

I have heard of a gentleman whose son had gone abroad, and being anxious to know how he was, he went to consult one who had this faculty, who told him that that same day, 5 a-clock in the afternoon, his son had married a woman in France, with whom he had got so many thousand crowns, and within two years he should come home to see father and friends, leaving his wife with child of a daughter and a son of six months behind him. Which accordingly was true. About the same time two years he came home, and verified all that was foretold.

The diarist John Pepys also took a keen interest in the subject of second sight and, like Aubrey, got himself correspondents who supplied him with information. His fellow-writers were Lord Reay, of Durness in Sutherland, and Lord Tarbat, whose descendants became the present Earls of Cromartie. Another contemporary involved in the correspondence was Robert Boyle, the eminent scientist. In one of the letters, Lord Reay mentions

the truth of the story about my grandfather's footman, and find it literally true; as also another, much of the same nature, which I shall give you an account of, because I have it from a sure author, a friend of my own, of unexceptionable honesty, to whose father the thing happened, and he himself was witness to it all. John MacKay, of Didril, having put on a new suit of clothes, was told by a Seer that he did see the gallows upon his coat, which he never noticed; but some time after gave his coat to his servant, William Forbes, to whose honesty there could be nothing said at the time, but he was shortly after hanged for theft, with the same coat about him, my informer being an eye-witness of his execution and one who had heard what the Seer said before.

I have heard several other stories, but shall trouble you with no more than what happened since I last came into the country. There was a servant woman in Mindo Aubrey's house, in Langdale on Strathnaver, in the shire of Sutherland, who told her mistress that she saw the gallows about her brother's neck, who had then the repute of an honest man; at which her mistress being offended, put her out of the house. Her brother, nevertheless, having stolen some goods, was sentenced to be hanged the 22nd August 1698; yet by the intercession of several gentlemen, who became bail for his future behaviour, was set free (though not customary by our law) which occasioned one of the gentlemen, Lieutenant Alex. Mackay, to tell the woman servant that she was once deceived, the man being set at liberty, she replied, he is not dead yet, but shall certainly be hanged, and accordingly he, betaking himself to stealing anew and being catched, was hanged the 14th Feb., 1699.

The peer also mentions an offer made to him by a seer to 'obtain' the gift second-hand:

There is a people in these countries surnamed 'Mansone', who see this sight naturally, both men and women, though they commonly deny it, but are so affirmed to do by all their neighbours. A Seer with whom I was reasoning on this subject finding me very incredulous in what he asserted, offered to let me see as well as himself. I asked whether he could free me from seeing them thereafter, whereto he answering me he could not, put a stop to my curiosity. The manner of showing them to another is thus: the Seer puts both his hands and feet above yours, and mutters some words to himself, which done, you both see alike.

Lord Tarbat in his letter to Robert Boyle stated some instances of which he knew:

being affirmed of several of great veracity, I was induced to make some inquiry after it in the year 1652, being then confined to abide in the North of Scotland by the English usurpers. The more general accounts of it were that many Highlanders, yet far more Islanders, were qualified with this sight; that men, women and children, indistinctively, were subjected to it; and sometimes age, who had not had it when young, nor could any tell by what means produced . . . There were more seers in the Isle of Lewis, Harris, and Uist, than any other place . . .
    I was once travelling in the Highlands, and a good number of servants with me, as is usual there, and one of them going a little before me to enter a house where I was to stay all night, and going hastily to the door, he suddenly started back with a screech, and fell by a stone, against which he dashed his foot. I asked what the matter was, for he seemed to be very much frighted; he told me very seriously that I should not lodge in that house, because shortly a dead coffin would be carried out of it, for many were carrying it, he was heard to cry. I, neglecting his words, and staying, he said to others of the servants he was very sorry for it, and that what he saw would surely come to pass; and though no sick person was there then, yet the landlord, a healthy Highlander, died of an apoplectic fit before I left the house.

After the close study of the subject, as evidenced in the letters he had received, Pepys declared: "I little expected to have been ever brought so near a conviction of the reality of it."

The tour of the Hebrides undertaken by Samuel Johnson and James Boswell in 1773 yielded more evidence of second sight. Despite the good Doctor's penchant for prejudice against all things 'Scotch', when he was given information on the subject of second sight, he "listened to all the fables of that nature which abound in the Highlands; and though no one fact was so well vouched as to command its particular belief, he held that the thing was not impossible; and that the number of facts alleged formed a favourable presumption." Johnson seemed to be impressed by the fact that "By pretension to Second-Sight, no profit was ever sought or gained." As a final word he says: "I never could advance my curiosity to conviction; but came away at last only willing to believe."

About half a century later, and into the middle decades of the nineteenth century, more instances of the occurrence of second sight were given a public airing, this time by Dr John Kennedy, minister of the Free Church in Dingwall from 1844 to 1884. He was well known and admired and accepted as one of the most accomplished of men, establishing a reputation which gave the weight of his testimony to the genuineness of so many remarkable instances of comparatively modern predictions actually fulfilled. His father was a seer. Dr Kennedy's instances are, as he says, "indubitable facts", and goes on, perhaps anticipating the sneers of the sceptics

> A little careful thinking on the subject might help one to see that, by means of the written word, under the guiding hand of His Spirit, the Lord may give intimations of His will in a way very different from the direct inspiration of prophecy, and that ends are served by such communications if His mind that make it far from improbable the Lord may have given them—for thereby His servants are encouraged, their hands are strengthened in their work, and proof is pressed on the consciences of the ungodly, that the true Israel of God are "a people near unto Him". And it is to simple and uneducated people, unable to appreciate the standing evidences of the Gospel, we might expect the Lord to give such tokens of His presence with those who preach it. The improbability of such things, to the minds of some, is owing to their own utter estrangement from the Lord. This is not the only secret, connected with a life of godliness, which is hidden from them.

The instances of second sight quoted by Dr Kennedy are given the stamp of truth, not only because of his cloth, but because many of those involved with the gift, either directly as seers, or indirectly as witnesses, were men who were strong in their religious convictions, who, with little compunction, would reject superstition and the like out of hand, but were willing to give credence to the existence of the gift of second sight, not merely because the "hand of the Lord" was seen in its various expressions, but because they perceived that man was possessed of mental faculties which were latent in the ordinariness of life but became manifest in those who, by some reason, were able to prove the existence of these faculties by their gifts. Nor was the acceptance by the Free Church seen in the same light as the Christianising of pagan elements in order to obtain converts, as was the case when the early missionaries began to introduce Christ to the natives in the early centuries A.D. There was no need of such basic conversion, only the use of it to convince the doubting Thomas that indeed the Lord moved in mysterious ways and was therefore eligible for acceptance by all who believed in salvation through Grace.

Once, while preaching on a Sabbath, the minister of Killearnan, while in full flight of oratory, suddenly paused and, in a subdued and solemn voice, said: "There is a sinner in this place, very ripe for destruction, who shall this night be suddenly summoned to a judgement-seat." The next morning, neighbours saw flames issuing from a hut, not far from the meeting-house, which was occupied by a woman notorious for her immorality, and in which, when they were able to enter, they found the charred bones of its miserable tenant. The same minister was credited with foreseeing the Disruption of 1843. When preaching in the church of Ferintosh in 1829, he announced: "This crowded church shall yet become a place into which none who fear the Lord will dare to enter . . . not long before this change takes place, I shall be removed to my rest, but many who now hear me shall see it." From that period till his death, his anticipations were more and more vivid. The coming crisis seemed to emerge before his eyes, more and more distinctly, out of the mist that lay on the future, and that hid its secrets from the eyes of others. In the event the minister, who had always enjoyed excellent health, suddenly took ill and within three days he was dead. Shortly afterwards, the Church in Scotland erupted into factions and the minister's words came to pass.

One Highland seer who has been overshadowed by the Brahan Seer was the Revd John Morrison, a minister of the parish of Petty, near Inverness. He is, in the Highlands at least, as well known for his prophecies as is the Brahan Seer, particularly in that they have been taken into part and parcel of the religious traditions of the whole north and west. The prophecies had, by the end of the nineteenth century, taken their place alongside the instances of Dr Kennedy, and thus have given the existence of the 'gift' as a basis for credence. Many of Morrison's prophecies are similar to those credited to the Brahan Seer and refer to happenings that were to occur in the near or distant future. In the case of Morrison's predictions, however, these are more distinctly authentic than those of the Brahan Seer in that, being a verifiable historical person, his utterances were recorded in both oral and literary traditions and were thus taken as further proof of the ability of certain Highlanders to operate on a plane which easily warped time and brought the future into the eye of the present.

After one of his strong sermons to his parishioners, he suddenly exclaimed: "Ye sinful and stiff-necked people, God will, unless ye turn from your evil ways, sweep you ere long into the place of torment; and, as a sign of the truth of what I say, Clach Dubh an Abhainn, large though it be, will be carried soon, without human agency, a considerable distance seawards." There was nothing so unlikely to happen, yet that stone was actually removed some twenty-six years afterwards and carried out to sea a distance of 25 metres. The following is an extract from *Anderson's Guide to the Highlands*:

> On the south side of the bay of Petty an immense stone, weighing at least eight tons, which marked the boundaries between the estates of Lord Moray and Culloden, was, on the night of Saturday, the 20th February, 1799, removed and carried forward into the sea about 260 yards. Some believe that nothing short of an earthquake could have removed such a mass, but to more probable opinion is that a large sheet of ice, which had collected to the thickness of 18 inches round the stone, had been raised by the tide, lifting the stone with it, and that their motion forward was aided and increased by a tremendous hurricane which blew from the land.

Mr Morrison is credited with predicting the evictions that took place in the parish of Petty:

> Large as the Ridge of Petty is and thickly as it is now peopled, the day will come, and it is not far off, when there will be only three smokes in it, and the crow of the cock at each cannot be heard, owing to the distance, at either of the others. After a time, however, the lands will again be divided, and the parish of Petty become as populous as it is at this day.

The first part of this prediction had occurred by the late decades of last century. The second part may now be in the process of fulfilment, for Ardersier, a former fishing village fallen on sore days, is now the centre of an oil-rig construction site which has attracted a vast number of workers and their families into the area.

One well-known instance of Morrison's occurred when a number of women from Fisherton, in the parish, had gone to Inverness to sell fish. Before returning home they invested some of their proceeds in liquid refreshment and were the worse for wear when they passed by Morrison's manse. Morrison went out to meet them, carrying a fiddle and, on seeing him, the women asked for a tune. He complied and in no time the women were enjoying a happy dance at the roadside. His elders, however, frowned on his conduct, to which rebuke Morrison said: "How could I refuse to play a tune for the woman who asked me to do so? The holy angels themselves will before long tune their harps for her. It would be better than a thousand worlds to hear the melodious music in the midst of which her soul will before this day week pass into glory." This woman took ill and died a few days after.

Morrison referred once to the clergyman who would succeed him in the church of Petty: "Colin John Morrison is laid in his grave, you will get a stammering Lowland minister who will neither have English nor Gaelic." His successor in fact had only very imperfectly acquired his Gaelic and scarcely any person could understand what he tried to say in that language; his English was on a par with his Gaelic.

Morrison predicted the conversion of many of his parishioners to his church, and in particular the ways in which they came to the altar for communion, after leading dissolute lives.

When, in such a short survey of Highland second sight, the Brahan Seer, Coinneach Odhar or MacKenzie, is asked to come forward to take his place, it is tantamount to requesting a ghostly shade to occupy a niche designed to be filled by an historical character whom documented evidence has proved to have, in his time, lived, worked and died. This seer is surrounded by shadows, mists of tradition and uncertainty as to whether he ever existed in the larger-than-life character with which the seer is credited in popular mind and memory. One school of thought suggests that Coinneach Odhar was a minor prophet who, in the fluid decades of the seventeenth century, was given credit for many prophecies he himself did not utter. The accretions of tradition, longing for a permanent home, attached themselves, almost by popular choice and acclaim, to this man, who has no acceptable documentary evidence of his existence, and enlarged to his present-day proportions. Yet—the seer has just sufficient evidence of his existence to tantalise the probable and push it, however unwillingly, into a very small domain of the possible.

Coinneach Odhar, Kenneth MacKenzie, towers head and shoulders above all other Highland seers. Though many of his sayings were no more profound than those of other seers, there remains a hard core of prophecies which is both remembered with deserved awe, and awaited with some apprehension for the fulfilment of those yet to come to pass. The earliest written reference to him is found in the Bannatyne History of the MacLeods (1832) at Dunvegan, which represents him as being a Lewisman. Some forty years later, Hugh Miller, the Cromarty stonemason and respected geologist, mentions in his *Scenes and Legends of the North of Scotland* (1874) that the seer was a field labourer near Brahan Castle, Ross-shire. The most detailed account of Coinneach Odhar may be found in Alexander MacKenzie's *The Prophecies of the Brahan Seer* (1899), which is a collection of oral tradition and folklore concerning his life, prophecies and death. Born of the MacKenzies in Baile na Cille, in Lewis, the seer received his gift of prophecy while a child. Later he moved eastwards to Brahan Castle where he worked on the Seaforth estate during the time of the third Earl of Seaforth, after the Restoration. Such a man, forthright in speech as his visions required him to be, eventually offended Isabella, Countess of Seaforth, who had him arrested and tried for witchcraft; he was burned to death at Chanonry Point, near Fortrose, some time between 1665 and 1675. It was just before his death that he uttered the famous prediction of the fate of the House of Seaforth which was to come true in uncanny detail many years later.

There is, however, in an otherwise well-documented century, no direct evidence that Coinneach Odhar ever existed. Like a frightened shadow, he lives in folk history, tradition and legend, flitting from prophecy to prophecy, consolidating his reputation and becoming clothed with a credence that has lasted to the present day. Research during the past decade or so, conducted by Gaelic scholars, indicates that the figure known as Coinneach Odhar is nothing more than a character created by popular belief on to which, like harpies, the products of 'Anon' have clung to produce a figure of substance. But when that has been said, there still remains a corpus of prophecy, away from the popular source, which defies all available research techniques to prove that they were created *ex post facto*, or were the result of a lively intelligence aware of possibilities, undreamed of in a contemporary context, but which were hard realities in their own time. Leonardo da Vinci could well have laid claim to have been a seer, a foreteller of things to come, because he was able to extrapolate from a contemporary state of knowledge to a stage far into the future where he envisaged commonplace items in our times, such as aeroplanes. What Alvin Toffler in his book *Future Shock* calls "the scientific trajectory" may well be accessible to many. In 1865 a newspaper editor told his readers: "Well-informed people know that it is impossible to transmit the voice over wires and that, were it possible to do so, the thing would be of no practical value." Less than a decade later, the telephone erupted from Mr Bell's laboratory and changed the world. The historic flight of the Wright brothers was badly reported in newspapers because the Press believed that what was claimed for them was impossible.

Whether Coinneach Odhar existed or not is beside the fact that Highland folk tradition has preserved some remarkable instances of prediction, many uncannily accurate in the time of their fulfilment. Some predictions credited to Coinneach Odhar are echoes of similar predictions made by other seers. The Islay seer, Am Fiosaiche Ileach, pronounced: "The day is coming when there will be a bridge on every burn and a white house on every headland in Isla." This must be compared with the saying of Coinneach Odhar: "A ribbon on every hill and a bridge on every burn." Again the Islay seer is credited with: "The time is coming when the sheep's tooth will take the coulter of the plough out of the ground in Isla"; from Coinneach Odhar: "The day will come when the jawbone of the big sheep will put the plough on the hen roost." One might even go further to discredit both Coinneach Odhar and the Islay seer by quoting Thomas the Rhymer: "The teeth of the sheep will lay the plough on the shelf."

Of the family of Clanranald of the Isles, Coinneach Odhar foretold: "The day will come when the old wife of the footless stocking (*cailleach nam mogan*) will drive the Lady of Clan Ranald from Nunton House. "The MacDonalds of Clanranald were the chief family in Benbecula. It was at Nunton that Flora MacDonald and Lady Clanranald dressed up Prince Charles Edward as Betty Burke. The direct line of the family eventually died out. The prediction was supposed to be fulfilled when a certain old lady known as Mrs MacDonald, Cailleach nam Mogan (*mogan*: a footless stocking, a form of primitive footwear) took over Nunton which was then occupied by her descendants long after the Clanranalds had fallen on hard times.

Other prophecies include: "The day will come when a laird of Tulloch will bury four wives in succession but the fifth will bury him." This has happened, last century, when the prediction, current before the laird concerned was first married, saw its fulfilment. "The natural arch, or Clach Toll, near Stoer Head in Assynt, will fall with a crash so loud as to cause the laird of Leadmore's cattle, twenty miles away, to break their tethers." In 1841 the arch did indeed fall and caused such a noise that Leadmore's cattle, which had strayed close to the scene of the fall, stampeded home in fright.

Concerning the Urquharts of Cromarty, Coinneach Odhar predicted: "Extensive though their possessions in the Black Isle are now, the day will come—and it is close at hand—when they will not own twenty acres in the district." This has happened literally. The Battle of Culloden, on 16 April 1746, is the theme of another of the Brahan Seer's predictions:

> Oh, Drumossie Moor, my heart is aching for thee, for the day is coming when thy black wilderness will flow with the best of Highland blood. I pray to God that I may not be spared to witness that day for it will be a fearful time. Heads lie lopped off in the heather; limbs are severed and lost; mercy has altogether deserted mankind while brother savages brother. Red coats are stained black with blood, red blood chokes the flower of the clans. The roar of the great guns has woken the dead in hell while the living weep in the glens. Children rise up against children, old men cut out the hearts of their companions. Oh God, oh Culloden, I am dying with your dead; I am stricken with your injured. Let me die before that day, oh let me die.

The prophecy was made a century before the battle occurred.

One remarkable prediction takes in some centuries of future Highland history, with some elements already reckoned to be fulfilled:

> There is a day coming when the jaw-bone of the big sheep will put the plough into the rafters and no man will drive cattle through Kintail. The sheep will become so numerous that the bleating of one shall be heard by another from Lochalsh to Kintail. You will not see it, but your children's children will see it when they are forced to flee before the march of the great white army, and the mountains will see it as I am seeing it now. After that, another day is coming when the sheep will be gone and so well forgotten that a man finding a jaw-bone in a cave will not recognise it or be able to tell what animal it belongs to. Strange merchants will take away the land of the great clan chiefs and the mountains will become one wide deer forest. The whole country will be utterly desolate and the people forced to seek shelter in faraway islands not yet known. Then will come the time of the horrid Black Rains. They will kill the deer and wither the grasses. Weep for the mountains and for what they will see in that day; weep for the wilderness of the Gael. After that, long after, the people will return and take possession of the land of their ancestors.

This prediction is remarkable because it foresees the history of the Highlands from the time of the evictions and the coming of the 'big sheep', the purchase of vast estates by English merchants and their conversion from sheep runs to deer forests The evictions and clearances caused Highlanders and their families to emigrate to New Zealand, Canada, America and Australia, places that were surely unknown to Coinneach Odhar. There has been much speculation as to the meaning of the "Black Rains". In the present-day involvement with North Sea oil, there is the temptation to regard oil as the agency which would "kill the deer and wither the grasses". To date these things have not happened and, indeed, it is difficult to envisage in what way oil could directly cause these effects; unless the industrial effluents from such operations as refineries might produce the necessary elements to see the fulfilment of the seer's prediction. A more chilling thought, however, is that the killing of deer and the withering of grass is well within the capability of radioactive fallout. Whether this might be the product of some future international and global warfare is open to conjecture; if it might be the result of a really serious accident in the atomic energy plant at Dounreay, in Caithness, then the seer might well be credited with the sight of a future event which is well within the realms of the possible.

Many of the seer's predictions are reckoned to have come true, such as the "fire and water" running through the streets of Inverness—what else but electricity and public water services? However some predictions seemed ridiculous in their content. Concerning the MacKenzies of Fairburn, the seer predicted that they would lose their entire possessions and their branch of the MacKenzie clan would die out completely. This might have been a fair prediction to make; however, the seer went further: "The great castle of Fairburn will stand uninhabited and forgotten and a cow will give birth to a calf in the top chamber of the main tower." At the time this prophecy was made, Roderick MacKenzie, the fifth Laird of Fairburn, was one of the richest and best respected chiefs in Ross-shire. He entertained lavishly in his castle and was waited on by liveried servants. The line was, however, to die out with Major General Sir Alexander MacKenzie of Fairburn who died unmarried in 1850. The castle had been left to rot for some time prior to this and by 1851 it was being used as a barn by a local farmer who used the tower to store hay. One of his cows who was in calf at the time followed a trail of straw up the winding staircase to the turret room and, being unable to get down again, was forced to remain there until the calf was born. This prophecy was so well known in the district that a special train was laid on from Inverness to Muir of Ord to allow curious sightseers to see the fulfilment of the prediction for themselves.

About Strathpeffer, the Mecca of Victorians who regarded the village as Scotland's answer to Bath, Coinneach Odhar said: "Uninviting and disagreeable as it is now with its thick crusted surface and unpleasant smell, the day will come when it shall be under lock and key and crowds of health and pleasure seekers shall be seen thronging its portals in their eagerness to drink the waters." By the nineteenth century Strathpeffer became a holiday and health resort.

There are many traditional versions of the last encounter between Coinneach Odhar and the Countess of Seaforth which led to the seer's prediction of the fate of the house of Seaforth and, as a consequence of his utterance, his own death by burning at Chanonry Point, near Fortrose. The general account is that Seaforth being in France, his wife sent for the seer to ask if he could tell what Seaforth was doing at that moment. In reply Coinneach Odhar said that the chief was well and merry. The insistence of Lady Seaforth to know more forced the seer to disclose that Seaforth was in the agreeable company of a French lady. The disclosure displeased Lady Seaforth and she had the seer committed for trial. It was then that Coinneach Odhar uttered the prediction that has become the hall-mark of the gift; no other prediction has ever received the attention of generations of Highlanders and scholars alike:

> I see far into the future where lies the doom of the House of Seaforth. MacKenzie to MacKenzie, Kintail to Kintail, Seaforth to Seaforth, all will end in extinction and sorrow. I see a chief, the last of his house, and he is both deaf and dumb. He will be father to

four fine sons, but he will follow them all to the grave. He will live in sorrow and die in mourning, knowing that the honours of his line are extinguished for ever and that no future chief of MacKenzie shall ever again rule in Kintail. Lamenting the last of his sons, he shall sink in sorrow to the tomb and the last of his possessions shall be inherited by a widow from the east who will kill her own sister. As a sign that these things are coming to pass, there will be four great lairds in the days of the last Seaforth. Gairloch shall be hare-lipped; Chisholm shall be buck-toothed, Grant shall be a stammerer and Raasay an idiot. These four chiefs shall be allies and neighbours of the last Seaforth and when he looks around him and sees them he will know that his sons are doomed to die and that his broad lands shall pass to strangers and his race come to an end.

This is undoubtedly the most famous of all the prophecies credited to Coinneach Odhar and the one which has caused the greatest wonder and speculation. There is no possible chance that the prophecy was made after the event, for at least three writers of excellent reputation knew about it when the last Earl had two sons alive and in good health. These writers were Sir Humphrey Davy, Sir Walter Scott, and Mr Morritt of Rokeby. When the last chief was, by his extravagance, forced to sell part of Kintail, the chief's tenantry offered to buy the land for him so that it might not pass from the MacKenzies. At this time one son was still living and there was no prospect of the succession dying. However, he, a man of great promise who represented Ross in Westminster, died suddenly and the prophecy was fulfilled. True to the seer's prediction, the four lairds of Chisholm, Grant, Raasay and Gairloch were all deformed in the way described.

The last laird, Francis Humberston MacKenzie, was not born deformed, but became stone deaf after an attack of scarlet fever as a boy which eventually ended in a complete inability or reluctance to speak. Most of his communication was done in writing. Of his four sons, the eldest died in infancy, the second died young, the third died in 1814, and the youngest died in 1813. His six daughters included Mary who was the widow of Admiral Hood. She later married a man called Stewart and inherited Brahan. It could be said that she was responsible for the death of her sister Caroline, for she was driving the pony trap when its horse bolted and Caroline was killed. In 1815 Lord Seaforth himself died, the last of his line. One by one the remaining estates were sold, first the Island of Lewis, then Kintail, the church lands of Chanonry, the Barony of Pluscardine, and even Brahan Castle itself, of which nothing now remains save a stretch of plain grass and some large trees.

Predictions have been made within the last century, or the fulfilment of predictions claimed to have been made earlier; these still form a topic of conversation in these modern and disbelieving times. In the autumn of 1914 a ship was requested to change her course and make for St Kilda to warn the islanders that Britain was at war with Germany. The captain duly held off the main island of Hirt and lowered a boat for the shore. No sooner had the boat scraped the pebbles of the beach at Village Bay when the crew was met by the islanders who asked how the war was going. Astonished, the captain asked how they knew and suggested that another ship had broken the news of hostilities to them. The islanders replied that visions had been 'seen', involving fighting between "our men and men in grey uniforms". The islanders did not know what country was involved in the war. They said that visions of heavy losses on the British side were also seen. A seer on the island had 'seen' the death of Queen Victoria long before a ship visited the island to bring news of the event, though there is some doubt about this vision.

During the 'thirties of this century an old man, walking home to Laxdale from Stornoway, Lewis, claimed he had 'seen' a group of people stooping over the body of a small boy at the south-eastern end of Laxdale Bridge. He reported that he felt that the boy had yet to be born and that he (the old man) would be dead and buried long before the event. Years later a small boy was killed by a motor lorry. Two women were in the vicinity of the same bridge when they 'saw' a mixed crowd of soldiers and civilians. Suddenly they heard a volley of gunfire, which frightened them so much that they scuttled for the nearest house. A fortnight later a high-ranking local army officer died in Stornoway. On the day of the burial the coffin, drawn by gun carriage, as far as the Laxdale Bridge, was transferred to a horse-drawn hearse, destined for a rural cemetry. As the transfer was completed, soldiers in the party fired a gun-volley to salute the departed soldier.

One of the Brahan Seer's prophecies contained a reference to a black horseshoe as a sign of world-wide catastrophe and this is claimed to foretell the Hitler war, during which the resurfacing of the North Uist ring road was left incomplete on its northern side, thus presenting, in a bird's-eye view, a horseshoe of black tarmacadam. The following is an account of a man with second sight in the Newtonferry district of the island some years ago. He was the local postman who one day arrived at the house of the local vet in a state of acute nervous exhaustion. He was clearly in no fit state to continue his round and, after he had gained some of his senses, he explained that in rounding a particularly dangerous corner beneath a rock bluff he had 'seen' lying at the roadside the remains of a smashed motor cycle and the badly mutilated bodies of a young man and woman. About a year later one of the worst road accidents in the island's history occurred at that same spot when, on a black night, a young honeymooning couple were killed outright when their motor cycle skidded.

CHAPTER 4

Ghosts

THE GHOST HAS A FIRM PLACE in the traditional beliefs, both past and current, of the Highlands and Islands and is a manifestation which displays peculiar, almost parochial tendencies. The ghost must be defined in the Highland context: a spirit either of the dead or of the living. If a spirit of the dead, the manifestation is a spirit body from the past making its appearance for some reason, usually to warn of some impending disaster. If the ghost is a wraith of the living, then the manifestation is that of some person close to the viewer, or else is that of a person undergoing some personal crisis, usually death. However, there is a third member of the ghostly species: the wraith of those as yet unborn at the time of sighting, which usually appears to those gifted with second sight. Thus, far from being a simple spirit, the ghost, in the Highlands at least, must be regarded as a manifestation which can represent the past, present and future, merely requiring an interpretation of a warped time-scale to place it in its contemporary setting, which latter, of course, is difficult except to an experienced seer.

The general instances of paranormal manifestations in this chapter will no doubt stir in the minds of most readers memories of similar or other types of happenings either within the context of their own experience, or of stories conveyed to them by friends and acquaintances. It is generally believed that the incidence of the 'unexplained' is much higher than one might be led to expect in a society such as ours which is so technology-oriented, and one in which belief in one or other of the established religions tends increasingly to be the exception rather than the rule. That this is so must firstly indicate that there are severe and practical limits to the known areas in which the average human being operates; but that outside these limits, which in many cases are merely perimeters of belief, there exists a dimension involving time—perhaps an elevated mental plane on which only those with special assimilative and participatory gifts can operate. Regularly one reads in the Press accounts of the experiences of ordinary people who, in a certain environment, created by a number of contributory and inter-related factors, have made contact with 'something' which was quite unexpected and outside the normal well-established patterns of life and living.

The Highland ghost is a complex being, reflecting history, ethnic origin, the character of the region, and personal experience. The other-world of the Celtic British once reflected the dreams of ancient warriors; it was a place of happiness, of continuous feasting and love-making; warfare occupied the residual energies of its occupants. This place was the Celtic heaven. The other place, to which all outcast Celtic souls were relegated, was typically inhospitable and tenanted by demons, giants and ghosts, and in which there was no peace at all. What can be called the 'Celtic ghost' has certain affinities with the Roman and Greek ghost, which is reasonably acceptable in view of the close relationship by locality and descent that existed between the three races. There is, of course, very little evidence to support this. However, the descriptions of the funerals of the early Celts and the rites of burial point to a somewhat more realistic belief in a future life than had either the Greeks or the Romans; the actual records of belief (such as the mone-tary loans that were given on condition that they should be repaid in the next world) give strength to this view. Caesar wrote: "Their funerals are magnificent and costly, considering their civilisation; and all that they think was dear to them when alive they put into the fire, even animals; and shortly before this generation, the slaves and depen-dents that they considered to have lived were burned along with them in the regular performance of funeral rites."

Diodorus, Caesar's contemporary, says: "For among them the opin-ion of Pythagoras prevails, that the souls of men are immortal, and in the course of a fixed number of years they live again, the soul entering another body. Accordingly, at the burial of the dead, some cast letters addressed to departed relatives upon the funeral pile, under the belief that the dead will read them." Another writer confirms Diodorus: "They burn and bury along with the dead whatever is of use to them when alive; business accounts and the payment of debt were passed on to the next world, and there were some who, of their own free will, cast themselves on the funeral piles of their relatives, expecting to live along with them."

Many old Irish legends point to the conclusion that the Celtic dead had ghosts of a more substantial character than either Classical or modern ghosts possess. The many tales of the Isles of the Blest (Tir nan Og), where an earthly paradise existed, argue that the dead lived in bodies of a very sensuous nature and of an earthly kind. The heroic tales present but one or two cases of ghosts actually coming back to earth; but these are not disembodied spirits in any sense of the term. These ghosts are about as glorious and golden as when they lived and moved among men. Three such appearances are recorded: Cuchullin's ghost, conjured up by St Patrick, to meet King Leogaire, who promised to embrace Christianity if the Saint could raise Cuchullin. There was the ghost of Fergus, raised by the saints of Erin, to recite the heroic tale, Tain Bo Cuailnge, in the seventh century when it was discovered that excellent epics had been lost to living man. In the same century, Caoilte was raised to decide a historical dispute between the poet Forgoll and a semi-supernatural king named Mungan (who was, however, said to be none other than Fionn himself resuscitated). These apparitions are all similarly characterised and described in great detail in the tales and all indicate the substance of the ancient Celtic ghost.

The Highland ghost has tended to appear before those who were possessed of a certain type of personality; the personality of the seer is a particularly important factor in the effective materialisation of a spirit. That this is so is seen in some instances when a ghost appears in a certain manner. Some ghosts are at once understood to resemble certain persons from the striking likeness of the one to the other; it is not an uncommon thing for the seer to speak to the ghost, under the impression that the party recognised in the apparition is addressed. The ability to see ghosts runs in families. In one brief survey of instances of ghost sightings, more than one-third were seen by members of one family, or by people who were closely related by the same blood. A friend of the writer casually accepts the frequent appearance of a harmless and gentle female spirit as being an aspect of her own, more substantial, life.

The stories about ghosts of the dead are as numerous and varied as one might expect. Many hauntings seem to have occurred with a particular purpose: to put right some wrong; to inform the living of something left undone; to warn of impending disaster; or, rarely, to exact some kind of revenge for a wrong done in the spirit's lifetime.

The wife of a fisherman in Sleat, Skye, was left a widow and was in no little distress as her husband had passed on without leaving any indication as to whether or not he had left any money which she could use to tide her over the early days of her misfortune. One night, while a storm raged outside the thick walls of her cottage, she saw her husband's ghost enter the room, clad in dripping oilskins. As she watched, quite unable to utter a word, the apparition crossed the floor of the room, in the direction of the fireplace. There the figure paused. Then, with a slow and deliberate movement, he made as if to remove a stone. He turned and, with a final gesture of farewell, he disappeared from her sight. After she recovered from her initial shock, a strong sense of curiosity made her examine the fireplace carefully. Surely, she found a loose stone which she removed, to find in the exposed cavity a considerable sum of money: her late husband's savings of which she had known absolutely nothing. In death he returned to help her in her time of need.

Sandwood Bay, some five miles south of Cape Wrath, in north-west Sutherland, is well known for its ghostly associations. The Bay itself is a seven-mile stretch of sand dunes. Though bleak in wintertime, it is a beautiful spot in the summer months and has become something of a Mecca for tourists seeking some place off the beaten track. The Bay and its environs are the haunting ground of a ghostly seaman. He has been sighted many times, but, when an investigation is made, there are no traces of footprints in the sand which would betray the presence of something more substantial than a ghost. Once, two men from nearby Oldshoremore were on the beach gathering driftwood. Suddenly, out from nowhere, the figure of a sailor in uniform appeared and commanded them to leave his property alone. Terrified, the two men dropped their load and fled. Some time later a farmer from Kinlochbervie was out in the vicinity of the Bay with some of his men on the lookout for stray sheep. Darkness was beginning to fall before all the animals were rounded up and, as the moon came out, the men noticed a tall man on the nearby rocks. Thinking it was one of the local men they went towards the figure; but as they drew near to him they realised that he was a stranger and looked like a sailor. A few steps nearer and the figure disappeared.

Several weeks after this incident a severe storm caused an Irish vessel to go aground close by Sandwood Bay; a number of bodies were washed ashore among which was one recognised as the person seen in spirit form. Since then there have been many instances of the ghost, particularly round about Sandwood Cottage, a building that has been untenanted for many years. Campers have been disturbed by noises coming from the cottage, and anyone taking to the cottage for shelter is usually disturbed by sensations of being pushed into the ground and suffocated.

Spirits wander about the surface of the earth for many years with a desire to unburden themselves. Many years ago a carrier for the district of Ness, in the north of Lewis, was making his way home from Stornoway. He had to pass the village of Galson, near to a large slab of rock where a pedlar was murdered and buried. The carrier was on foot, leading his horse, when, as he approached the stone, he felt a presence close to him. Looking round he saw a figure dressed in the fashion of a man of half a century previously. The spirit asked the man to stop. The latter, however, had a clean cold fear on his heels and started to run. But the ghost laid a hand on his shoulder and guided him to the stone slab where he was forced to sit and hear out the details of the crime. How much time he spent sat there the carrier did not know, but when the light of dawn broke on the horizon causing the ghost to fade away, he felt the staying hand slowly lift from his shoulder and was glad to be off. The pedlar's words were with him for many a day after that.

The Revd Thomas MacKay was minister in Lairg, Sutherland, until he died in 1803. He wore during his lifetime full clerical dress. One summer's day in 1826 two young girls were sitting in the manse dining room when they heard a step advancing to the door. At once the door opened and they saw, standing in the doorway, a thin, old man, dressed in black, with knee breeches and buckles, black silk stockings and shoes with buckles. With a stare that took in everything in the room, he stood for a few moments and then walked out. After they had recovered from their astonishment, the girls mentioned the incident to the resident minister who, curious to know who the visitor was, searched the house, but found no one. Later enquiries yielded the information that it was the ghost of the previous minister, returned presumably to take a look around his earthly charge.

In 1869 a man from the parish of Farr, in Sutherland, had occasion to post a letter. It was a distance of over two miles to the post office, most of the way being across some hills. As he approached the main road, he was taken hold of by some unaccountable fear and a feeling of imminent danger. So alarmed did he become that he thought of turning back, though the day was bright and calm. Suddenly he was confronted by a man well known to him, whose face and hands were a mass of congealed blood. He asked the injured man what had happened to him, but was waved off. He noticed, however, that one of the man's fingers was broken. He was then told that the injured man had left his mother's house two days before, intending to visit some friends in a neighbouring village, and took a path which ran along the cliffs so as to shorten his journey. At the lower end of his mother's croft his foot slipped and he fell to the bottom of the rocks. He stated further that he had lain there for two days and two nights and that once he had heard, carried by the wind, his mother's voice as she spoke to a neighbour. Then the ghost vanished.

Startled and half-frozen with fear, the other hurried on his way to the Post Office where it was seen that he was in distress and suffering from some kind of mental anguish. He told his story and, accompanied by the local minister and some others, the postmaster went to the spot indicated. There they found the lifeless body of the man whose mysterious appearance had so terrified the other. One side of the head was badly injured and the middle finger of the left hand was broken. Everything in fact was as described an hour before the body was discovered.

Some miles south of Stornoway is a spot which was the preserve of a persistent ghost who appeared as suddenly as he would disappear. A number of years ago a man's body was discovered in the vicinity. The find consisted of human remains, clothing and personal objects. Due to the action of the peat acid, the bones were reduced to the consistency of rubbery seaweed. The woollen cloth required several washings and then treatment with lanolin to replace the lost fats in the material. The skeleton was that of a man between twenty and twenty-five years of age. The opinion of the Department of Forensic Medicine, in Edinburgh University, was that "the appearances seen in the posterior part of the right parietal bone are consistent with, and indeed suggestive of, a localised depressed fracture such as would result from the impact of an object having a defined striking surface. The position of this fracture would be consistent with a blow wielded by a right-handed assailant attacking from the rear". In short, the young victim had been murdered. The clothing was dated *c.* 1700.

Local tradition was that two youths attending a school at Stornoway went to the moors on a bird-nesting expedition. They quarrelled and one of them felled the other with a stone. Realising his deed, he fled south to Harris, whence he made his way to the mainland and took up a seafaring life. For years afterwards the ghost of the victim was often to be seen in the vicinity of a grey rock. The body in the peat of Amish Moor was so close to the traditional scene of the almost legendary crime that it is not unreasonable to link the events of crime, ghostly hauntings and eventual discovery of the remains.

Ghosts of the living, though a different type of manifestation, are no less terrifying and disturbing to those who see them. Phantoms of the living have received from the Society for Psychical Research a scientific or quasi-scientific explanation by the invention of the word 'telepathy'. Its etymological force is 'feeling at a distance' end is intended to denote the mysterious influences and impressions which one mind is able to exert upon another mind, apparently without the usual means of communication, and even at a far distance. The modern term of 'extra-sensory perception' is an aspect of this subject which is undergoing serious investigation at seats of higher learning, such as in Edinburgh University. Experiment has tended to prove that telepathy— the supersensory transference of thoughts and feelings from one mind to another—is a fact of nature (supersensory is defined as being independent of the recognised channels of sense). Many verified testimonies prove that phantasms (impressions, voices or figures) of persons undergoing some crisis—especially death or impending disaster—are perceived by their friends and relatives with a frequency which mere chance cannot properly explain.

The distinction between spirits of the dead and those of the living has been known and accepted for many centuries. In the Highlands the word 'ghost' is applied only to a spirit of the departed, while the spirit of a living person is described in such terms as 'wraith' and the Gaelic *samha* (likeness) or *tamhasg* (apparition). It is an interesting fact that in the Highlands there are more stories about the ghost based on the wraith idea than on the ghost as a spirit of the dead. Most of the appearances of wraiths indicate the impending death of the person whose spirit has been seen, or that the person was in some kind of crisis which so stressed the mental and subconscious to the extent that the personality had parted company with the body to appear before some relative or friend. There are people today who can tell of their strange ability to 'come out of themselves' and leave their bodies in a spirit form. The experience is one in which there exists an almost ecstatic freedom from the stresses undergone by the earth-bound body.

Typical is the story of the old man sitting with a young boy on a felled tree beside a steep track in a quarry near Ballachulish. The two were in deep conversation when the old man jerked the boy to one side and took himself over to one side of the trunk. The boy stared at the old man in some understandable confusion while the latter rose to look fixedly in front of him and saying: "The spirits of the living are strong today!" He then told the boy that he had seen a mass of rock fall from a nearby height to kill some of the quarry workmen. The accident, as foretold, occurred the following day at the spot where the pair had been sitting.

Phantom funerals are the most common form of apparitions of living people and stories about them are endless. Typically, two men are walking along a road when suddenly one pushes the other to the side of the road; or else one sees the other become seized with a constriction in his breathing and struggling as though to get through a dense crowd of unmoving people. There was once an unwritten rule of the road in the Highlands: never walk in the middle of the road for fear you may find yourself in the middle of a phantom funeral party and be taken along with them.

There is a fairly large body of accounts of ghostly lights and sounds which defy rational explanation, and which includes such subjects as death divination and second sight. Usually the appearance of lights indicates the death or impending death of someone either known to the seer or some person in the community. One man, not given to story-telling for its own sake, took serious views about omens seen either by himself or by others. On several nights the sounds of a strange four-oared boat were heard coming from the opposite shore of Loch Erisort, Lewis, close by his home. This, he claimed, presaged a death and the inevitable occurred within two months with the arrival of two boats, each bringing a coffin to the village.

The late Alasdair Alpin MacGregor tells the story of a doctor from Edinburgh who was holidaying at an inn at Broadford in Skye. After supper he decided to take a turn outside before settling down for the night. Walking along the shore in the half-light of the evening he noticed a glow out in the bay. At first he took it to be a flare lit by some fisherman in a boat. But then he noticed that the light was travelling too smoothly for that explanation. In addition, it was travelling at a pace which indicated that it was no ordinary kind of light. Gradually the light came nearer until it touched the shoreline—then went out. The next thing of which the doctor was aware was the form of a cloaked woman, with a child in her arms, hurrying across the sand in front of him. The glimpse he had was only a fleeting one, because the woman vanished in a moment.

Returning to his lodgings, the doctor asked his host for an explanation. In reply he was told of a shipwreck which had occurred several years before in which a woman and child had been cast ashore, both dead, at the spot where the doctor had seen the strange light. The light has been seen in modern times.

Father Allan MacDonald, parish priest of Eriskay at the turn of this century, recorded many aspects of folklore and traditions of the island and neighbouring South Uist. In particular he recorded many valuable instances of ghostly, or at least inexplicable, happenings which defied attempts at rationalisation.

Both ghostly lights and sounds feature in his notes. He relates:

> Towards the end of August 1888 I was called to attend a dying woman at South Lochboisdale. After administering the rites of religion, a crew and boat were procured. As we were nearing Strom Dearg, one of the rowers drew attention to a light playing on the shore just at the spot where we had embarked. It continued for some time, but its appearance did not cause much astonishment, only we could not imagine what objects any person would have in being in such a spot at such a time. We thought the dying woman would live till morning, but when the boatmen returned home, the woman was dead, and they were told she was dead just at the time we should have been approaching Strom Dearg. The men spoke of the light and made diligent enquiry if any person had been to the shore, and it was found that no person was there. The coincidence was remarkable.

CHAPTER 5

Functional Folklore

IN COMMON WITH OTHER societies throughout the world, forced to rely on initiative and the careful assessment and applications of natural resources for the maintenance of health and for the progression of their cultures, communities in the Highlands and Islands of Scotland developed a dependence on Nature, to the extent that their lifestyles and the lives of the individual members of a community reflected this relationship in the lore of plants, animals and birds. Some of the dependence on Nature was based on vital necessity: many plants could be used to cure ailments which might otherwise be left unattended for the want of skilled help in the form of a doctor. The occult properties of herbs in particular were well known and, indeed, in the past decade or so have staged a comeback to counteract the increase in the use of chemical-based drugs which often have long-term harmful effects on the human system. Many herbs are given properties by popular belief: their efficacy in cures depended on sympathetic magical elements which, in their turn, relied on the belief that what happens to one thing is to some extent dependent upon what happens to something else with which a magical link has been forged (for example, an object being blessed before its use in a curative ritual). Cereals are of prime importance in any folk herbal, as is evidenced by the far-flung belief in the corn-spirit, often personified either by a human or an animal, which was sacrificed, or apparently sacrificed, to come to life again, thus symbolising the renewal of the crops and indicating the hope of continued fertility and fruitfulness. Oats have for long been cultivated in the more northerly parts of Europe; hence porridge is the national dish of the Scots. It was symbolised by the oats-mother, the oats-bride, and also by a stallion, a goat, a sow and a wolf. The physical property of the cereal is important in the maintenance of the health of the body. Its occult property was contained in the belief that it could also uphold the spiritual welfare of man, accomplished through the development of rites carried out at the initial preparation of the ground, the subsequent sowing, the harvesting and the baking of a cake from the first of the flour product. Each stage in the route from germination to consumption was underwritten by a ceremony until a complex corpus of ritual was developed for religious observation by each succeeding generation in a community.

Fruit and nuts also played a part in maintaining life and spirit in the body. Apples are said to have followed acorns as the chief food for primitive man; but, apart from their nutritive value, they are associated with many beliefs, with a frequent occult reference to love. At Michaelmas and Halloween, the apple was a feature in ceremonies heavily drenched with awesome significance. The nut, and particularly the hazel nut, was a feature of such festivals as the Celtic Samhainn, in which it was used as an important element in divinatory practices.

It is, of course, in the realm of healing that plants have assumed an importance which might seem preponderous to the modern mind, surfeited as the latter is with manufactured cure-alls available over a chemist's counter. But when one considers that professional medical aid was not available to the common folk, but only to those in the higher social orders, and even then was of doubtful quality, it can be appreciated that recourse to traditionally proved and accepted forms of plant life was the only way out of problems created by disease or other physical disorders. In time, diseases became associated with extraphysical causes and remedies and, as a consequence, cures were accompanied by rituals, the meanings of which were often obscure, diffused by time, even to the performer. Herbs are the bases of folk medicine and have been from before the time of Christ. At one time a knowledge of herbs was claimed as a charter to practice by physicians who had not studied anatomy, physiology and the clinical subjects offered by medical schools, and who eventually became known as herbalists.

Often described as superstition is the ritual of plucking plants at certain times of the day, night or season of the year. Yet, albeit unknown to those who practised folk cures and who followed rituals according to tradition passed from mother to daughter, and father to son, there was both rhyme and reason for this. It has long been believed that the growth of vegetation varies with the phases of the moon. Lunar rhythms have been proved to exist in plants, animals and in human beings. Experiments have shown that there is an increase in growth with the waxing of the moon. There is also a yearly cycle, growth decreasing on the whole towards the winter months. Both factors must be taken into account. In fact, in December, the usual increase towards the time of the new moon does not occur, and there is a remarkable acceleration of growth before the Easter full moon. During the fortnight before the latter, additional growth more than compensates for the usual effects of the waning moon.

It can be suggested that much of the herbal lore found in Gaelic tradition is derived from the times of the Druids. Though these priests exist for us in a shadowy history, full of assumptions, there are certain elements of what is known of the Druidic order which have seemingly found a continuity from these ancient times to ours in the present day. One example is the attention paid by the Druids to plants; the mistletoe, endowed with mystical significance as was its host oak tree, is an instance of a carry-over from an older time so that today Christmas is nothing without its mistletoe. To each god in Celtic mythology there was dedicated one or more special plants. The original Gaelic alphabet was also in correspondence with a list of trees. The alphabet consisted of seventeen letters, to which was later added the letter 'H', though it is used mainly for aspirative purposes. The list is:

Ailm (elm), Beite (birch), Coll (hazel), Dur (oak), Eagh (aspen), Fearn (alder), Gath (ivy), Huath (uath or white-thorn), Iogh (yew), Luis (rowan), Muin (vine), Nuin (ash), Oir (spindle-tree), Peith (pine), Ruis (elder), Suie (willow), Teine (furze), Ur (heath).

The plants which figured in the lore of the Gael served either as a food or else were used for their known healing properties, the latter being administered in various forms: liquid to be drunk, or in an ointment base, severally, jointly, and often in concert with a ritual which contained some rhyme incorporating a supplication to a saint. The knowledge of the herbal and medicinal uses of plants is of very long standing; it spans, more than likely, some millennia of tradition and factual-based lore, handed down in families who were regarded with respect in their communities and often given special positions and privileges in return for their services. The herbalists provided many basic concoctions, and housewives supplemented these by recipes based on plants. These latter included such dishes as *cal dheanntag* (nettle broth), and *cal duilisg* (dulse broth). In spring the first tender shoots of the common nettle were minced and boiled, sometimes with a little oatmeal. It was regarded as being one of the best spring diuretics, apart from its being nourishing. *Duilseag*, while it could be eaten raw (and indeed it warded off the hunger-pangs of many during the evictions of last century), was much more palatable and digestible when cooked. As a food and diuretic it was much prized by our maritime ancestors.

Other edible plants included various species of sorrel (*rumex: sealbhag*), still used in salad mixtures, the roots of the creeping cinquefoil, or silverweed (*Potentilla anserina: brisgean, or barr brisgean*). The roots are tuberous and, eaten raw, have a slightly nutty taste. When roasted, however, they have a pleasant mealy flavour. The tuberous or everlasting bitter vetch (*Orobus tuberosus: corr-meille*) has long, branching, underground roots, strung with nodulous lumps at frequent intervals. These, after they are dried, were chewed as wild liquorice. Far less deleterious than common chewing-gum, the taste continues in the mouth long after the last shred is chewed. The taste is both acid and sweet and so never palls. In times of scarcity the plant was used as a food, as Lightfoot indicates:

> The Highlanders have a great esteem for the tubercules of the roots; they dry and chew them to give a better taste to their whisky. They also affirm that they are good against most diseases of the thorax, and that by the use of them they are enabled to repel hunger and thirst for a long time. In Breadalbane and Ross-shire they sometimes bruise and steep them in water, and make an agreeable fermented liquor with them, called Cairm. They have a sweet taste like the roots of liquorice, and when boiled are well-flavoured and nutritive, and in times of scarcity have served as a substitute for bread.

The range of wild plants used for the cure of ailments is very wide and embraces those which, consumed in quantity, would prove fatal; but when these are administered in small doses, in line with current medical practice, they prove beneficial to the patient. No doubt many plants, poisonous in significant quantities, were introduced into community pharmacopoeias as the result of trial and error; but once their worth was proven, they became firm ingredients in remedies. With the advance of learning, the healing properties of plants came to be classified into a *materia medica* which, in the course of time, came to include remedies from the animal and mineral kingdoms. But the vegetable element in medicine persisted as the most important; indeed, notwithstanding that many of the simple remedies used in past times are now discredited, they remain as firmly embedded in the popular mind as being able to perform their traditional roles now as then. In Scotland, the great exponents of medical skills included the MacBeths or Beatons. They flourished in the western Highlands and Islands from the beginning of the fourteenth century. They committed much of their knowledge and learning to records and some of their Gaelic medical treatises are among the earliest extant Gaelic MSS. The family was to be found in Mull, Skye, Islay and the Uists. Martin Martin mentions that when the Spanish Armada treasure ship "the Feorida", was blown up in Tobermoray Harbour, Dr MacBeth, the famous physician of Mull, was then sitting on the upper deck, which was blown up entire, and thrown a great way off; yet the doctor was saved, and lived several years after."

Writing about Skye, Martin Martin mentions the cures wrought by an "illiterate empiric", Neil Beaton, "who of late is so well known in the isles and continent [Scotland] for his great successes in curing several distempers, though he never appeared in the quality of a physician until he arrived at the age of forty years, and then also without the advantage of education. This 'empiric' was credited with "cutting a piece out of a woman's skull broader than a half crown, and which restored her to perfect health". It was inevitable, with centuries of lore behind them, that the knowledge of the Beatons became disseminated throughout the region and absorbed by those with lesser claims to fame than the Beatons, and who became, in their own communities, the medical facility to whom all resorted.

The plants used for healing were divided into vulneraries, febrifuges, emetics, cathartics, irritants and tonics. In the first group, the vulneraries, are included cancer-wort (*Geranium robertum: Lus-an-eallain*), used for skin affections; Kidney-vetch (*anthillis Vulneraria: Meoir Mhuire*), long held to be efficacious in the cure of cuts and bruises; Golden-rod (*Solidago virgaurea: Fuinnseadh coille*), credited with the virtue of healing and joining broken bones; Wood sanicle (*Sanicula Europoea: Buine*), used in healing green wounds and ulcers; Yarrow (*Millefolium Europoeum: Earr-thalmhainn*), a potent styptic; Fig-wort (*Scrofularia nodosa: Lus-nan-cnap*), used in the cure of scrofula or King's Evil; and the highly regarded comfrey (*Symphytum officinalle: Meacan Dubh*). Old Culpeper, the famous sixteenth-century English herbalist, says of Comfrey: "Yea, it is said to be so powerful to consolidate and knit together that, if they but boiled with dissevered pieces of flesh in a pit, it will join them together again."

The second group, febrifuges, included the expellers of fever. Wood or dog-violet (*Viola canina: Brog-na-cuthaig*) was used in a concoction boiled in whey to allay fevers; white helleborine (*Epitatis latifolia. Ealabot geal*) cured colds in the head: blaeberry (*Vaccinium myrtillus: Lus-nam-broileag*) soothed pains; and house-leek (*Sempervivum tectorum: Lus-nan-cluas*) was used, mixed with cream, to put away earache.

Counter-irritants were used to reduce stubborn local pains among the best known were spearwort (a species of Buttercup, which had to be used with caution on account of its violent action, and was attended with dangerous effect when administered internally). Martin Martin mentions that the best healer of the blisters thus raised was a plaster of the sea plant *linnearaich*, a species of *Confervae*. Groundsel (*Senecio vulgaris: Crunnasg*) was used for cataplasms to produce suppurations.

Many plants were used as emetics, some of the more popular being fir club-moss (*Lycopodium selago: Garbhag-an-t-sleibhe*), effective but it had to be used with caution; and scurvy grass (*Cochlearia officinalis: Am Maraich*), which had a reputation as a valuable plant with medical properties of a corrective nature. The lesser meadow-rue (*Thalictrum minus: Ru Beag*) was a powerful cathartic.

Among the tonics and appetisers were lovage (*Ligusticum scoticum: Sunais*), much used in Martin Martin's time as a tonic and prompter of sluggish appetites, along with the gluttony-plant or dwarf cornel

(*Corpus succosia: Lus-a'-chraois*); and the dandelion (*Taraxacum leontodon: Am Bearnan Brighde*) which was, and perhaps still is, one of the most valuable ingredients in tonics and other medicines. Garden-sage (*Salvia officinalis: Saisde*) is remembered for its worth in healing in a Gaelic proverb: "Carson a gheibheadh duine bas aig am bheil saisde fas 'na gharadh?" (Why should a man die that has sage growing in his garden?) Delf-heal or heal-all (*Prunella vulgaris: Dubhan ceann-dubh*) was effective in removing all obstructions of the liver, spleen and kidneys; trefoil or bog-bean (*Menyanthes trifoliata: Tri-bhileach*) was a potent tonic, often administered regularly in the form of a tisane.

If the knowledge of plants and their healing properties was well known, so also was that of plants which were poisonous. Hemlock, with its long-standing classical reputation, had a number of names in Gaelic suggesting some aspect of the plant. Night-weed was well-known for its large black berries and their somniferous qualities; more dangerous was henbane (*Hyascyamus niger: Gabhan*), sometimes known as *Cuthach-nan-cearc*, "that which sets the hens mad". The juice of the petty spurge (*Euphorbia peplus: Gur-neimh*) was so caustic as to be used to destroy warts.

Perhaps it was inevitable, in the progression and development of the healing properties of plants, that medical knowledge came to be supplemented, and eventually complemented, with a belief in the magical properties of these same plants. Perhaps one or two failures, resulting from the wrong prescription for a particular illness, required some kind of guarantee that the applied remedy was to work success-fully. It is common knowledge that the early Christian Church humoured beliefs in the occult powers of plants, herbs and trees; but these beliefs, instead of being diminished by tolerance, grew in a body which assumed a new stature in folk lore and practice, by which time it had to be accepted with an even greater degree of tolerance. Yet, who is to say that the various chants, rhymes, runes and prayers said in accompaniment to the application of a remedy for a particular illness were not in themselves contributing to the success of the treatment? And the more so when these chants included supplications to saints, Biblical deities and even the Christ Himself? However, beliefs went further: deep into the realm of protection against spiritual ills and ailments. For instance, perforated St John's wort (*Hypericum perforatum: Caol aslachan Chaluim Chille*) was St Columba's favourite flower; he rever-enced it and carried it in his arms because it was dedicated to his favourite among the four evangelists, St John. It was in great vogue in former times as a charm against witchcraft and enchantment. Another name for the plant, *Allas Muire* (meaning the image or semblance of the Virgin Mary), made it a rather sacred plant. Agrimony (*Agrimonia rupatoria: Mur Dhruidhean*) reflected the association of the plant in the folk mind with the Druids, and its supposedly magical effects on spiritual troubles as well as diseases; it was used to heal a wide variety of ailments. The rowan tree (*Pyrus aucuparia*) was known by various Gaelic names: *Luis* (drink) and *Luis-reog* (a charm which used to be distilled into a spirit). Its presence beside homesteads all over the Highlands indicates, more then than now, the widespread belief that it was a charm against evil spirits. Lightfoot (1772) says the Highlanders believed "that any part of the tree carried about with them proves a sovereign remedy against all the dire effects of enchantment or witchcraft". The foxglove (*Digitalis purpurea*) had several Gaelic names associating the plant with the fairies, such as *Meuran sith* (fairy thimble). The yarrow or milfoil (*Achillea millefolium: Earrthalmhainn*) was an especially favoured plant with mystical properties. Young women cut it by moonlight with a black-handled knife, for use in a ceremony which was designed to yield the name of their true loves. As with the rowan, the ash (*Fraxinus excelsior: Uinnseann*) was credited with magical properties and used against charms and enchantments; it was used, too, against the effects of serpent bites (spiritually as well as materially). Pennant (1772) says: "In many parts of the Highlands, at the birth of a child, the nurse puts the end of a green stick of ash into the fire, and, while it is burning, receives into a spoon the sap or juice which oozes out at the other end, and administers this to the new-born babe."

The combination of the known curative properties of plants and the suggestive curative elements inherent in supplications to saints and other propitiative beings became firmly established in the large body of folk medicine in the past. Administered as 'medical spells' for diseases of both humanity and beasts, cures were, perhaps surprisingly, successful. Only on occasion were such ingredients used as bats' wings, dried spiders, and the like, so popular in the mind of the sceptic, not so much by genuine healers, who knew the tricks of their trade, but by quacks who imposed their will on their credulous clients, using tricks rather than traditional knowledge. Rather the bulk of cures were effected by the use of materials, with complementary chants, which gave to the user his or her necessary degree of credibility. There were other methods, however, which used inanimate objects such as beads and thread rather than natural, organic items. Relief for sprained ankles, dislocated joints and toothaches was obtained by reciting a chant and passing a bead across the affected part; or a thread of common worsted was knotted at intervals and, as each knot passed over the fingers, a line of a charm was said. These 'cures' are still practised in the Highlands, with some degree of success, though mainly with animals, which might be all the more significant because any possibility that auto-suggestion is involved is eliminated and the cure must 'work' on its own accord, in its own way and of its own volition.

Some cures are on record as authentic instances of the skill of the folk medicos. At the turn of the century a woman suffered from a rather prominent wen, which a neighbouring 'skilly woman' volunteered to remove for her. The remedy was simple: to walk over the moor to the medico's house, a distance of about two miles. When she reached it, she was told to sit down, quite still, while the skilly woman got ready a needle and knife. The needle was pointed at the wen and then, acting as if it were actually cutting the wen, the knife made motions of cutting it off. The ceremony was accompanied by an incantation, in Gaelic, repeated seven times. After a few visits, always with the same ritual, the wen slowly disappeared, to the mystery and amazement of all who knew of the cure.

Blood-staunching required a gift known as *casg fola*, or blood-stopping; any person with the gift could stop any bleeding at a moment's notice without medicines and appliances, but simply by the power of his word. It was, however, essential to know the name of the person to be cured, otherwise the charm would not work. There is on record the case of a lad in Wester Ross who cut himself badly, so much so that his friends feared that he would die with the loss of so much blood. They took him immediately to a local medico called Iain Ban. The medico tried but his charm failed to work. It was only when another in the community, a woman, came forward with the suggestion that there were grave doubts as to the lad's paternity, that the charm was administered again with the lad's correct name uttered, when the bleeding stopped.

Another case involved a girl in the neighbourhood of Inverness who had a tooth extracted, which then bled for several hours. Treatment given by a qualified doctor brought only temporary relief. A friend then contacted a local farmer, known to possess the *casg feola*, who immediately went into a closet and muttered a charm. The time was 10.15 p.m. Shortly he emerged and told the girl's friend to return as the bleeding had stopped. In a fit of disbelief, the friend returned—to find that, indeed, the bleeding had been staunched, shortly after ten o'clock. If there were no person with the gift in a district, natural means were used to staunch blood-flow, such as shepherd's purse, nettles, puff-balls, ribwort and spider's webs; but yarrow was considered the best agent.

It is, perhaps, but a short step from the application of concern for the ailments of one's fellows to concern for the natural and satisfactory progression of tasks designed to sustain life in and around the household, and to keep one free from both clinical and spiritual ills. Belief that one's life was overshadowed by unseen spirits which influenced the success or otherwise of human activity was widespread, and led to the build-up of a significant corpus of lore which, at first sight, might seem to be rank superstition but which, on careful scrutiny, reveals the close affinity of man with nature. This latter was a relationship which was encompassed by a simple and pure belief that all in Nature was for the common good and must therefore be treated with respect. If there were elements of the belief in animism, this was only to be expected in a society which regarded communion with Nature as a normal facet of everyday life; and if their view of Christianity was larded with a thick skin of these elements, who can say that the resultant religion, while incomplete in doctrinaire terms, was not more wholesome, in that it satisfied the basic need of humans for a channel through which spiritual satisfaction could be obtained?

The most significant collection of lore concerned with human activity, severally or in concert, is *Carmina Gadelica*. Now available in six large volumes, it was the lifework of Alexander Carmichael last century who, in the course of his duties and travels as a Revenue official, collected snippets of the residual oral Gaelic lore which was then extant but fast fading as the older generation died away and the succeeding generation preferred to concern itself with the more pressing contemporary problems of famine, disease and overcrowding in the congested districts of the Highlands and Islands. Many of the items of oral lore which Carmichael rescued from oblivion reveal the intense feeling for nature; even where this is expressed via a religious vehicle, some slight syncopation of an accepted belief in an otherwise caring and obedient society, there is no feeling of blasphemy or popular paganism. Rather it was something to be admired and, indeed, sought after: this simplistic view of life, surrounded as it was with material problems, yet was singularly the vehicle for spiritual peace. The following, one of many examples that could be quoted, is Carmichael's preface to a Prayer at Dressing, obtained from the wife of a crofter in Moydart:

> The woman said: My mother was always at work, by day helping my father on the croft. and by night at wool and at spinning, at night clothes and at day clothes for the family. My mother would be beseeching us to be careful in everything, to put value on time and to eschew idleness; that a night was coming in which no work could be done. She would be telling us about Mac Shiamain, and how he sought to be at work. If we were dilatory in putting on our clothes, and made an excuse for our prayers, my mother would say that God regarded heart and not speech, the mind and not the manner; and that we might clothe our souls with grace while clothing our bodies with raiment. My mother taught us what we should ask for in the prayer, as she heard it from her own mother? and as she again heard it from the one who was before her.
>
> My mother would be asking us to sing our morning song to

God down in the back-house, as Mary's lark was singing it up in the clouds, and as Christ's mavis was singing it yonder in the tree, giving glory to the God of the creatures for the repose of the night, for the light of the day, and for the joy of life. She would tell us that every creature on the earth here below and in the ocean beneath and in the air above was giving glory to the great God of the creatures and the worlds, of the virtues and the blessings, and would *we* be dumb!

Other prayers were said at rising and to accompany the various tasks involved in starting the household on their daily tasks. The fire was bestirred into flame; later, walking down to the shore, across the fields, and over to the hills, a short prayer, 'Ceum na Corach' (The Path of Right) was said as an individual act of supplication for protection against any ill that might occur during the course of the coming day. Even the simple act of going to the well to draw water was accompanied by a petition for safeguarding. If any member of a household was to make a visit to a neighbour, or to go farther afield, the journey was blessed. Work on the land and on the sea was subject to blessing and goodwill towards those who were to carry out the work. Herding, milking, warping, weaving, spinning, going to the summer sheiling, churning, were examples of crofting work made the more significant by the chants and prayers that accompanied them.

Occasionally the Gael's regard for Nature intruded into the quasi-religious domain in the people's lives. As Carmichael wrote:

The people addressed invocations to the sun, moon and stars. Men and women saluted the morning sun and hailed the new moon. The practice prevailed over the British Isles, nor is it yet obsolete, though now a matter of form more than of belief. The people hailed the morning sun as they would a great person come back to their land; and they hailed the new moon, "the great lamp of grace", with joyous welcome and acclaim. The sun was to them a matter of great awe, but the moon was a friend of great love, guiding their course upon land and sea, and their path wherever they went.

As the day ended the tasks needed to set the house and the household at rest were again subjected to ritual: the smooring of the fire and the invocation of protection before sleep.

Life, however, was not governed by the rhythm of days. The seasons, the months of the year, all contributed to the Gael's orchestrated life as he progressed from birth to death, participated in community affairs and enhanced his own life by courtship, marriage and parenthood. We are again indebted to Alexander Carmichael for the notices of ritual and ceremony surrounding the entrance of new life into the community:

> Birth and death, the two events of life, had many ceremonies attached to them. Many are now obsolete, and those that still live are but the echoes of those that were current in the past. When a child was born it was handed to and fro across the fire three times, some words being addressed in an almost inaudible murmur to the fire-god. It was then carried three times sunwise round the fire, some words being murmured to the sun-god. The first water in which the child is washed after it is born into the world, the bathing-woman puts a gold piece or a coin of silver into the vessel of water in which the child is being washed. And the woman does this for love of peace, for love of means, for love of wealth, for love of joyousness by day and by night, for grace of goodness, for grace of fortune, for grace of victory on every field.
>
> After the child is born it is baptised by the nurse; this is called 'baisteadh ban-gluin', the knee-woman's baptism. "When the image of the God of life is born into the world, I put three little drops of water on the child's forehead. I put the first little drop in the name of the Father, and the watching-woman say Amen. I put the second little drop in the name of the Son, and the watching-women say Amen. I put the third little drop in the name of the Spirit, and the watching-women say Amen. And I beseech the Holy Three to lave and to bathe the child and to preserve it to Themselves." By the Book itself! ear has never heard music more beautiful than the music of the watching-women when they are consecrating the seed of man and committing him to the great God of life. No seed of fairy, no seed of the hosts of the air, no seed of the world's people, can lift away the happy tranquil little sleeper for whom is made the beneficent prayer of the baptism; eye cannot lie on him, envy cannot lie on him, malice cannot lie on him.

Then, inevitably, came *Latha a'Bhais*, the Day of Death:

> The old people had a great desire for good weather at the death and burial of a person. It was a good sign that the elements should be at peace at that time. There were two reasons for this. If there was peace on earth it was a sign that there was peace in heaven and a welcome for him who had gone and that the King of all creatures was at peace with him and His own two mighty arms open to take the immortal soul home to Himself. And if there was peace on earth this gave opportunity to friends and kindred to come to the burial and take farewell of the body in the natural earth and in the grave of the fathers. If the weather was bad it was

a sign that God was wrath. And the bad weather kept friends and kindred from coming to the burial. If the day was wet or misty it was a sign that the King of the elements was pouring wrath on the earth. If the day was black, dark and stormy it showed that God, the Creator of all creatures, was pouring the black wrath of His grief on the soul of him who had gone. If it was a day of snow this was a sign that the white wrath of God was upon the bruised soul that had gone over the black river of death.

There was, however, the chance of the *Bas Sona*, the Happy Death, which was the result of a departed soul having being confirmed in his faith, reconciled with his Maker, before darkness closed the eyes. The *Bas Sona* was, in fact, something looked to with eagerness by all whose times were running out, so that they could participate in the gentle easing of life out of their bodies with a clear conscience and with no fear of the after-death consequences of their acts in life in the realm of the unknown.

It is, perhaps, a matter of no great surprise to know that it is accepted by folklorists of international repute that there is no greater corpus of work songs than exists in Gaelic. Being locked away in a minority language, though an indigenous tongue of the British Isles, it has not been exposed to general awareness by many of those who might otherwise have appreciated it. Even so, the work of a few Gaelic scholars today has at least shed light on the traditions of the Highlands, though in translation. Considering that the vast amount of material extant was carried through the centuries in folk memory and manifested only through oral tradition, with literary help only towards the end of last century, one might expect that what remains today as witness to the life and lifestyle of the Gael in the past would be mere tatters, poor shadows, and faint echoes of what once was. The opposite is the case and, happily, the accumulations of centuries of tradition bear witness to the fact that Gaelic society developed along a characteristic path and preserved the worth of what had gone before.

The work songs cover the whole range of domestic and community activities and contain elements of tradition that have since disappeared from other forms of lore. The songs take in such work as weaving, spinning, waulking, shoemaking, herding, milking, churning, driving cattle, fishing, collecting seaware, and the tasks associated with land use. Often invocations to the saints, chiefly Columba, are made while the work was being blessed or started with a blessing, thus strengthening the success of the task. With such goodly company, what work was never brought to a successful conclusion? What venture, such as fishing, could not bring home a sea-harvest when St Peter was in charge? Which of the many tasks performed by women were not assured of a satisfactory end when St Bridget was the subject of an invocation or supplication ?

As an example of the penetration of the light of naturalistic religion into the whole lifestyle of a Gaelic community, one can point to the Invocation for Justice, a want for justice:

> Thou shalt arise early in the morning and go forth afield. Thou shalt betake thee to a boundary stream that shrinks not in heat, in drought, in parching sun, in drouth of summer. And thou shalt dip thy face in the stream three times in succession. And after that thou shalt bathe thy countenance in the nine gentle rays of the sun. Thou shalt say thy prayer and proceed to the moot, and no matter nor might, between ground and sky, between heaven and earth, shall prevail against thee, shall have effect on thee, shall oppose thee, shall keep thee from what is thine.

It may seem that the life of the individual was heavy with concern to perform the right ritual, utter the right charm, observe the correct nuance of a sequence. But Carmichael reports that at no time in his travels in the Hebrides and on the west coast of Scotland did he meet with complaint. Instead, life, though burdened with material problems, was operated on that elevated plane which relegated such problems to a place of no particular consequence. Functional folklore provided the release and the escape; where and when it could not, it was then a matter of resignation. Life was for an allotted span in any case and could be borne with fortitude: an attitude which still pervades many a Highland and Island community today.

CHAPTER 6

Seasonal Lore

THE REFLECTION OF A PEOPLE'S beliefs, attitudes to ancient traditions, and their stances on matters affecting individuals in a community, or the community as a whole, is to be found in no surer mirror
than in the calendar of events kept throughout the year. The twelvemonth cyclic period in human lives, with its four internal changes, is
the hook on to which is hung the old clothes of one's ancestors, kept
up to date by shifts in emphases as the community's history is altered
by internal and external influences and events. Many of the 'days' kept
in the Highlands and Islands are now long forgotten; but documentary
records, and oral tradition, show that there was an intense interest in
their observance, for one reason or another, but not least to obtain the
propitiation of some saint, or revered historical or mythological figure,
for the welfare of the future.

Many of the major annual events, such as Beltane, Hogmanay, St
Bride's Day, and Midsummer Eve, were, and still are to some extent,
commemorations of the significant high peaks of earlier societies,
based on seasonal change, or turning points in the sun's career as it
rose and declined in respect to a community's horizon. The Christian
trappings which were laid over much older festivals, with their attendant rituals which might have offended those with a firmer grasp of
faith in the new religion, did much to preserve what had gone before.
But at the same time they introduced a shift of object and objectives so
that saints replaced idols, and tribal and mythological personages.
Like an old building newly consecrated, observances throughout the
year offered a convenient base for missionary work. That the new beliefs
were taken up with gusto is evident from the large corpus of written
material imped out by collectors of folklore and tradition from the
preservers of Gaelic oral tradition among the folk of the Highlands
and Islands. One of the most significant collections is *Carmina Gadelica*,
compiled as the result of many years of hard work and physical inconvenience by Dr Alexander Carmichael. As might be expected in the
collection, many observances are Celtic in character, but display the
overlaying of the influence of a greater God which pulled them out of

the natural rhythmic cycle of the Celtic year to the less apparent, and perhaps more transparent, cycle of Christian festivals. Even so, the foundations were well laid, and the old heartbeats can still be detected, vibrating on their characteristic Celtic wavelength which, as they always did, followed close on the heels of mother nature.

The two most important works which contain the bulk of information about Scotland's festivals and calendar events are *Scottish Calendar Customs* by Mrs M. MacLeod Banks, and *The Silver Bough* by the late F. Marian McNeill. Even the most cursory glance will reveal the thick weave of traditional belief and custom which has been part and parcel of Scottish life and living for centuries. In the Highland context, these calendar events and cyclic festivals are no less interesting; indeed, one might venture to say they are more interesting in that they not only reflect general Scottish stances to tradition but add an extra dimension of interest in that they are largely derived from the Gaelic-speaking areas of Scotland. While today these areas are now confined to perimeters of the north-west and western seaboard of Scotland, even a century ago the Gaelic boundary extended far south into Perthshire, Fife, Angus and highland Aberdeenshire. Thus, the residual traditions now available for research are derived from almost half of Scotland's area. The following short tour through calendar observances reveals the substance of the lore of the Highland folk.

Lent was *Am Traisg*, or *trasgaidh*, the time of fasting. This was an important date in the calendar for a number of reasons. In past years, time was counted by church festivals, the priest being the timekeeper for the parish; there was a calendar at the beginning of his service-book, so the community came to him for their chronology. In many parts of the Highlands which remained Catholic long after the Reformation, the socket of the Paschal candle, and even the candle itself, was used to advertise the approach of significant times; this reckoning succeeded the older folk-reckoning which was based on the same luminary, the moon. One Gaelic mode of calculation was "Seven short weeks from Shrove-tide, *Inid*, to Easter, *Caisg*".

Shrove Tuesday is the eve of Lent (Gaelic: *Inid*, from the Latin, *initium*; thus, *Di-Mairt Inid*). When the full moon of Shrovetide comes a few days after St Bride's Day, it is known as *Inid Bheadaidh*, forward *Inid*, and is supposed to bring an evil time for the greedy man in the lean days after Easter. Shrovetide was always reckoned to be the "First Tuesday of the Spring Light", heralding the new moon in spring. It was, too, a time for prognostication; for nut-burning and marriage divination, for putting symbolic articles in brose and cakes specially prepared for the occasion. It was an important time for the saining of cattle: juniper was burnt before the cattle, with other rites, to keep the cattle free from harm. Matrimonial brose was a savoury dish generally

made of the bree of a fat jigget of beef or mutton. Before the bree was
served on a plate, a ring was mixed with the meal, which it was the
aim of every eater to win. After the brose came bannocks, enough to
satisfy all the young people at the feasting and with sufficient symbols
shared out to make all happy; some of the bannocks were 'Dreaming
bannocks', with which a little soot was mixed. In baking the bannocks, the baker had to remain silent until they were cooked; one word
could destroy the divination properties of the whole batch. One cake
was given to each person, who then quietly slipped off with it to bed;
sleeping with one's head on the bannock would provide one with a sight
of a future partner.

At this season cock-fighting was popular in the Highlands. Towards
the close of the eighteenth century the salary of the schoolmaster at
Applecross, in Wester Ross, was 200 merks Scots: "he bath no perquisites
but the quarter's payment of 1s. 6d. [7½p] for English scholars, and
2s. 6d. [12½p] for Latin and arithmetic, and the cock-fighting dues,
which are equal to one quarter's payment from each scholar".

The first day of Lent, Ash Wednesday, was *Di-ceudaoin* na *Luaithre*,
Wednesday of the Ashes. Another name was *Inis*, sorrow.

The sixth Sunday in Lent is Palm Sunday, *Di-Domhnaich Slatpailm*.
The sun was believed to dance at its rising on this day. On the morning
it was the custom to go to the top of a hill or rising ground to catch a
sight of the sun as it came above the horizon. The Sunday before
Easter was 'The Day of the Big Porridge'. As this day fell at a period
late in spring, and particularly if the winter's winds had failed to cast
up a sufficient supply of seaware on the shores, it was time to resort to
extraordinary means to secure the necessary manure for the land. A
large pot of porridge was prepared with butter and other good ingredients, and then taken to the headlands near creeks, where seaweed
was normally to be found. A quantity of the *brochan* was poured into
the sea from each headland, accompanied by certain incantations and
in consequence of which acts, it was believed, the harbours became
full of seaware. The theory was that by sending the fruit of the land
into the sea, the sea would, in return, send back some of its own
resources. This device was resorted to only in late spring and in stormy
weather. In Iona, however, the ritual was always performed on the
Thursday before Easter. In Lewis in olden times, mead or ale was poured
into the sea:

> O God of the sea
> Put weed in the drawing wave
> To enrich the ground,
> To shower on us food.

Other ceremonies, with similar intentions, were carried out in other sea-girt parts of the Highlands. Farther inland, efforts were made to use the advantages of this auspicious day for the protection of cattle from diseases for the next twelvemonth. Staves were cut from the service tree, to be used on the first day of May, duly adorned with herbs, which were fixed above doors.

Good Friday was of particular significance in the lives of Highland folk. Many taboos were recognised. No iron, for instance, had to come into contact with the ground. It was expressly forbidden to plough on Good Friday, though potatoes could be planted with a wooden dibble, and the ground raked over with a wooden-toothed rake. So great was the aversion to doing any ploughing that there was, in some areas, a permanent prohibition on every Friday. If a burial had to take place, the grave had to be opened on the previous day, and the earth settled over the coffin with a wooden shovel. No blacksmith could work on Good Friday, because the nails of the cross were said to have been made on that day. Many other community tasks were also forbidden, such as the sowing of seed and spinning flax. It was a popular article of belief that those born on Good Friday had the power of seeing spirits and of commanding them.

Easter Sunday is *A' Chaisg*, the death day of the eggs, on account of the large number of eggs disposed of on this day. The eggs were invariably rolled down slopes, the significance of the act varying with the locality. Divination, using eggs, for future husbands or wives, was performed in Arran. In Harris, the number of eggs which survived their roll to the bottom of the slope indicated the extent of good luck to befall their owners. Easter Sunday was another day on which the sun could be observed dancing. From the Uists:

> The people say that the sun dances on this day in joy for a risen Saviour. Old Barbara Macphie at Dreimsdale saw this once, but only once, during her long life. And the good woman, of high natural intelligence described . . . what she saw or believed she saw from the summit of Benmore: "The glorious gold-bright sun was after rising on the crests of the great hills, and it was changing colour— green, purple, red, blood-red, white, intense-white, and gold-white, like the glory of the God of the elements to the children of men. It was dancing up and down in exultation at the joyous resurrection of the beloved Saviour of Victory". To be thus privileged, a person must ascend to the top of the highest hill before sunrise, and believe that the God who makes the tall blade of grass to grow is the same God who makes the large, massive sun to move.

Whit Sunday was a legal term-day in Scotland generally. Ecclesiastical salaries, pensions and all dues were paid at this time, as they were at Martinmas. Removals to houses, or flitting to new houses, was carried out on Whit Sunday. In Sutherland the event was used as a calendar reckoning and to mark it a fair was held on the Tuesday of the term which derived its name from a wool manufactory, now long discontinued, called New Kelso, near Loch Carron.

Another movable festival was Harvest, the date being shifted according to the state of the weather and so was quite independent of any festival decreed to be observed by the Church. This time was of course autumn, either August or September. The beginning of the harvesting operations was at Lammas, when the season was believed to be propitious. The corn reaped in the Highland harvests, and which formed the background of so much folklore and custom, was chiefly oats. Oatmeal was an indispensable element in the harvesters' supper. The "meal and ale" of many a song was thickened with oatmeal to ensure a bountiful crop in the ensuing year.

But while the Church itself was a minor influence in the harvest observations, religion *per se* was prominent. The day the reaping began was a day of commotion and ceremonial in the townlands. The whole family went out to the fields dressed in their best clothes, to hail the god of the harvest. Laying his bonnet on the ground, the father of the family would take his sickle and, facing the sun, cut a handful of corn. Whirling the corn three times sunwise round his head, he would raise the *Iollach Buana*, the Reaping Salutation. The whole family took up the strain to praise the God of the harvest, who gave them corn, bread, food and flocks. During the harvest the people sang songs, as Dr Samuel Johnson noted on Raasay:

> I saw the harvest of a small field. The women reaped the corn, and the men bound up the sheaves. The strokes of the sickle were timed by the modulation of the harvest-song, in which all then voices were united. They accompany, in the Highlands, every action which can be done in equal time, with an appropriate strain, which has, they say, not much meaning; but its effects are regularity and cheerfulness.

The end of the harvest was charged with a symbolism as full of meaning and portent as was the beginning. The most important rite was centred round the last sheaf to be reaped, which was known by different names, but usually Maiden, *Cailleach*, Lame Goat, according to the locality where it was cut. In Islay, Kintyre and in the Hebrides, the last sheaf was the *Cailleach* (old woman); while in other parts it was the Maiden (for example, in Mull). While the ceremonies associated with the last sheaf varied from district to district, they had many common elements. The description of the ceremony on Bernera, Lewis, might be taken as typical:

In Bernera, on the west of Lewis, the harvest rejoicing is called "Cailleach" from the last sheaf cut, whether in a township, farm or croft. Where there are a number of crofts beside each other, there is always great rivalry as to who will have the first Cailleach. Some even go out on a clear night, after their neighbours have returned so that they may run her before the other crofters. More neighbourly habits, however, usually prevail, and as each finishes his own he goes to the assistance of another, till the whole township crop is cut. As they still shear with the hook, the rivalry is often great. When all have finished, the last sheaf is dressed up and made to look as like an old woman as possible. It has on a white cap (currachd), a dress, a little shawl over the shoulders fastened with a sprig of heather, an apron turned up to form a pocket, which pocket is stuffed with bread and cheese, and a hook (sickle) is stuck in the string of the apron at the back, the idea being that in this attitude and costume she is ready to join in the harvest toil.

At the feast which follows, the Cailleach, dressed as described, is placed at the head of the table, and as the whisky goes round, each of the company drinks to her, saying: "Here's to the one that has helped us with the harvest". When the table is cleared and dancing commenced, she is taken out by one of the lads present, who dances with her, and should the night favour it, the party may go outside and march in a body a considerable distance, singing harvest songs, the old wife accompanying them, carried on the back of one of the men. When the Harvest Home is passed, the Cailleach is shorn of her gear and used for ordinary purposes.

The Cailleach represented a number of real fears and hopes. She was as much a symbol of future famine as she was also a symbol of success in winning crops from the land. She was a tutelary being, watching over the crops to ensure that they came to fruition. She resided in the last sheaf cut, her supervisory role being retained until the very last act in the fields; thus, the treatment this sheaf received governed the fate of the next season's crop. For instance, near Lochgilphead it was customary to offer a tuft of the sheaf to the horses on the first day of the following season's ploughing, as a *sainnseal* (handsel) for luck.

The other name for the last sheaf, Lame Goat (*Gobhar-Bacach*), had an evil inference. In Skye, the last sheaf cut on one man's croft was passed to another, not yet finished; in his turn he passed the sheaf to a third, and so on until the last man was presented with it. According to the district, the sheaf implied bad luck for the future; or else implied shame for being tardy in harvesting.

Divination was resorted to at harvest-time. In one area, when the reaping was finished the people set up a trial called *Cur nan Corran*, casting the sickles, and *Deuchair Chorran*, trial of hooks. This consisted among other things of throwing the sickles high into the air and observing how they came down, how each struck the earth and how it lay on the ground. From these observations the people augured who was to remain single and who was to be married, who was to be sick and who was to die, before the next reaping came round.

The practice of magic was bound up in the harvest ceremonies. When the *Cailleach* was offered round, its passage was accompanied by the recitation of certain words, one anxious observer, a chiel taking notes, complained: "They closed the door that I would not see or hear what was going on; but I was not in the house, I was just behind them, but she said the words so low that I did not hear her. That is the way with the whole of these, they do not wish anyone to get the words." What the observer failed to appreciate was that the words she failed to hear were intentionally spoken in low tones, for if a magical formula is to remain powerful its words must be kept secret except to the initiated. The desire to preserve secrecy is a good indication of the belief in the magical efficacy of the spoken word.

Harvest rites were finalised by both play and games, for children as well as adults:

> The ring dance was the common dance at the kirn, or feast of cutting down the grain, and was always danced . . . by the reapers of that farm where the harvest was first finished. On these occasions they danced on an eminence, in the view of the reapers in their vicinity, to the music of the Lowland bagpipe, commencing the dance with three loud shouts of triumph, and thrice tossing up their hooks in the air. The intervals of labour during Harvest were often occupied in dancing the Ring to the music of the piper who formerly attended the reapers. This dance is still retained among the Scottish Highlanders, who frequently dance the Ring in open fields when they visit the south of Scotland as reapers, during the autumnal months.

The festival of Beltane was of special importance, particularly in its connection with what was once popularly called 'fire worship'. The celebration of Beltane on the first of May was significant as a high time for the propitiation of the elements, particularly the sun, to influence the growing crops. Cattle were made to pass through the smoke of the Beltane fires so that they might be cleansed of any evil spirits which might bring them disease during the ensuing year. The *Teine Eigin*, the fire of need, was lit on this day—after all the fires in the community had been extinguished—and from it new house fires were rekindled. Deeply embedded in the festival was the belief that at this time, the welcoming of summer, there was a grand anniversary review of all witches, warlocks, fairies, wizards and other spirits and spirit controllers, to which new entrants were admitted. Such a congregation of evil was much to be feared and it was thus essential that every ritual was carried out in the correct manner: rowan twigs, tied with red thread and made into crosses, were inserted into door lintels; Beltane bannocks were baked and distributed to children.

Like its counterpart in the Celtic year, Samhainn, the origin of Beltane cannot be traced, like so many other notations in the year, to ecclesiastical sources. Like the names for February (*Faoilleach*, the storm month) and July (*Iuchar*, the hot month), they predate Christianity.

Beltane was essentially the opening day of the year, when the rigours of winter are finally cleared away and the months ahead show promise of warmth and fertility. Its arrival signalled a wide range of activities, such as releasing the cattle for their trek to the summer pastures among the hills (*the airidh*). A churning of butter was necessary, as was the making of a cheese, before sunrise on Beltane, to ensure that the fairies were kept away from the household produce. No fire was given out on this day (nor indeed on any other first day of a quarter of the year—*latha ceann raidhe*), for fear that the borrower might be given the power to spirit away milk from the lender's cows.

In Perthshire, boys going to the moors on this day kneaded a piece of oatmeal, one part of which was daubed black. The bread was then put into a bonnet from which each withdrew a piece. The boy who picked the blackened piece was obliged to leap three times through the flames of a fire. In other districts, herdsmen offered pieces of the cake to the fox, the hoodie crow. eagle and similar predators, with a request that they avoid their cattle charges during the year.

Samhainn, Hallowmass, is the first day of winter and was in some ways even more important than Beltane, for it was a time when the work of the year was drawing to a close and preparations had to be made for the coming coldness. In addition, the spirits which had blessed crops and flocks now required payment by the observation of ritual. All the fruits of the summer were gathered in and set aside until the following spring, to the accompaniment of both ceremony and play. The children gathered anything to hand for a bonfire, usually built on some rising ground and lit in the evening. The fires were called *Samhnagan*. There was one for each house and often it was an ambition to have the biggest. The sun, having done its work during the previous months, was now to be replaced by man-made heat and the fires represented this new reliance on self rather than on nature. Among the games played were those thought to have some divination element in them: to see who would be married in the following year, whether trade was to be fair, and what lay ahead in terms of life and death. Many of the methods used can hardly be classed as superstitious for they were more often devised for fun than from any belief in their efficacy; even so, some methods, with coincidental results, were given credence as to their power to predict the future and came to be rationalised and offered a place in a community's niche of folklore to be carried over and strengthened with each succeeding generation. Today, many of the customs of Hallowe'en owe their currency to these past activities.

The Celtic year, with its Christian accretions, was chock-full of important times. Apart from the movable feasts, these times were pinpoints in the twelvemonth cycle designed to mark out the days with a regular beat. Many of the present saints' days in the Highland calendar were no doubt Christianised, to offer an acceptable and palatable bridge between earlier beliefs and the newer offerings, which, often, had so much in common with what was intended to be phased out as 'pagan'. However, Christian missionaries did their work well and it is often with great difficulty that present-day calendrical observances are proved to have an ancient lineage.

The four seasons are known as *Earrach*, spring, *Samhradh*, summer, *Fogharach*, harvest, and *Geamradh*, winter. The final syllable in these Gaelic names is *radh*, a quarter or season of the year, a space of three months. The character of the seasons is described in an old Gaelic riddle:

> Four came over,
> Without boat or ship,
> One yellow and white,
> One brown abounding in twigs,
> One to handle the flail,
> And one to strip the trees.

The derivations of the names are interesting. Spring comes from *ear*, the head, front, or the east. In the naming of the four quarters of the heavens, the face, as in the case of the Hebrew names, is supposed to be towards the east. Spring, then, is the leading season of the year. The element *samh* in summer is the sun-season or quarter. It contains an element of the heaviness of summer, produced by excessive heat, and the deep feeling of almost luxurious lethargy which hot weather produces in man, beast and plants. In Tiree *samh* is the word used to describe the hazy appearance of the ocean. The element *fogh* in autumn contains the meanings ease, hospitality, sufficiency and abundance—surely a true indication of human expectations from the work and growth of the previous seasons. The root of winter, *geamh*, indicates a stiffness and a binding, appropriate descriptions of what winter is capable of doing: to imprison all things in ice and coldness and to slow down the heart-beats of life almost to a death-like stillness.

The computation of time by months and days of the month, as at present, was unknown to the Highlander of former days. Even nowadays, older folk tend to ignore such accuracy as "the 27th of June" and talk instead of so many days before or after a term-day or festival. For instance it was only recently that fishermen let go their hold of the fact that ling fishing on the west coast lasted from the middle of spring into the first five weeks of summer (the beginning of April to about 18 June). The names for Gaelic months tend to be derived from Latin, with some exceptions to show their ancient starting points predating Christianity.

February (*Am Faoilleach*—wolf month and dead month) is important for its first day: St Bride's Day, the first day of spring. At this time winter still rules, covering the earth with a shroud of late snow or else soaking it with the dampness of its cold, bone-chilling rains. This day is 1 February Old Style, or the 13th New Style. St Bride was, according to tradition, the first nun in Ireland. She built many monasteries and performed good works to become eventually Patroness of Ireland. But her influence was far spread and she appears in many places, cells and wells. St Bride's Day signals the day when the raven begins to build and the lark sings with a clear voice. White, in his *Natural History of Selborne*, noted that 14–17 February is the period during which the raven does indeed make attempts at nest-building.

March was the seed-time. The Gaelic word *Mhart* signifies a busy time; the month itself contains St Patrick's Day, which is the middle day of spring on which both day and night are of equal length. A certain sign of this day is held in the Hebrides to be a south wind in the morning and a north wind at night; this was supposed to be the saint coming from Ireland to see his flock accompanied by a favourable wind both coming and returning. It is of significance for its signal that the reviving influences of spring are now to be seen: "There is not a herb in the ground, but the length of a mouse's ear of it is out on St Patrick's Day".

Whistling Week occurs in the first week of summer; it is so called because of the loud whistling winds which often blow at this time. It is unlucky during this week to proceed with field and other outdoor tasks.

August is *Iuchar*, the hot month and the counterpart of February. As the first day of autumn it stands as a high point in the natural calendar. St Finan's Eve is the longest night in the year. The shortest day was 'The day of the three suppers' in Sutherland.

Other days observed include many named after saints. Indeed, no day escapes its association with some ecclesiastic, perhaps an indication of how keen missionary zeal was to flood the old systems of time-keeping with the new. But Highland memory created many other 'dates', such as the Year of the Big Sheep, when sheep made their first commercial appearance in the Highlands; and, in Tiree, the Year of the Silverweed Roots; which occurred shortly after Culloden and was a year when there was a great scarcity of food in the island.

The days of the Highland week were significant for certain kinds of work. Sunday (*Di-Domhnaich*) is a day of rest. Monday (*Di-luain*) is the key of the week (*Iuchar na seachdain*). It was always thought unlucky to begin any kind of work on Mondays, especially ploughing: "Work commenced on Monday will be too quick or too slow". It was, however, a good day for flitting, just as Saturday was the reverse. Tuesday, on the other hand, was a good day for ploughing; and if any part of the harness broke, this was regarded as an especially propitious omen. Wednesday was good for sowing seed. Thursday was the high spot in the week, being the Day of St Columba. Work started on this day was especially blessed, such as the beginning of weaving cloth and other domestic tasks. It was, however, particularly bad if Beltane day, the first of summer, fell on a Thursday:

> Thursday the day of benign Colum-cille,
> A day to take possession of sheep,
> To put cloth in warp, and settle cow on calf.

Friday was the most important day of the week and was attended by many rituals, a considerable number of which are derived from the fact that Friday was the day of the Crucifixion. "Friday is against the week", is an old saying, signifying that on this day the spirits of evil had more power than on any other. Iron was not allowed to be put into the ground, whether for ploughing, digging or for graves. It was not lucky to cut one's nails, sharpen knives, commence any work, count animals or go near the fire; it was a bad day for marriages, seamen and fishermen. On Fridays fairies were supposed to be able to visit men's houses and people were thus careful not to utter anything that might be taken in offence. The belief that the spirit world had an aversion to iron might explain why the ground was not to come into contact with the metal; nor was the sound of sharpening the metal pleasant to spirit ears. The origin can be reasonably placed in Christian belief: Christ was dead but was to rise again, the interregnum, however, being a time for spirit misrule; iron was a feature of the Crucifixion, with nails being made and knives sharpened for fashioning the stakes. Thus, Christianity was able to overlay a previous belief that iron was hated by the spirit world which might have derived from the time iron made it appearance as a weapon of war and control.

In Tiree, one way of getting an old woman into a rage was to count her chickens on Friday. This might be an echo of the time King David numbered the Children of Israel. Animals were not killed on a Friday, nor were they moved from one pasture to another on this day.

Saturday was left alone so far as those tasks that could not be finished by the end of the day were concerned, due to the interruption of the work by Sunday: "The warp prepared on Saturday will have the delay of the seven Saturdays upon it". "Saturday light goes seven times mad before it goes out" was an allusion to the belief that a new moon on a Saturday was deemed to presage a period of stormy weather. Saturday, however, was a welcome rest for the working man; "Alas! and alas! is Monday; but my love is Saturday."

The days of Yule were fully charged with import, including as they do Christmas, Hogmanay and the various saints' days. The seven days from Christmas to the New Year were called *Nollaig*. No work was done during them; rather folk gave themselves up to friendly activities and offering both words and deeds of goodwill towards neighbours. Christmas Day was *Latha Nollaig Mhor*, the Day of Big *Nollaig*, and the night before it was *Oidhche nan Bannagan*, the Night of Cakes. New Year's Day was known as the Day of Little *Nollaig*; its Eve was *Oidhche nan Calluinnean*, the Night of Blows.

Hogmanay was better observed than Christmas, mainly because of the former's place in the calendar: the old year was leaving its mortal coil and the new year was to be born to hopes of a new life, better prosperity and an improvement in the lot of whomsoever wished to have times better than those experienced in the departing year. Thus while Christmas was duly accepted for its message of hope, Hogmanay was of more immediate concern because it affected life and the material things around it. New Year's Day was preceded by *Calluinn*, which was observed by playing games, shinty being the most popular, and the preparation for a procession round the houses of the township. At each house a train of men and boys, though latterly the tradition was kept up by boys only, knocked on the walls of houses and, going sunwise, chanted a request for gifts. The main feature of the procession was that the leader's head was enclosed within the hide of a mart or cow, which was periodically struck like a drum by his companions. The 'gifts' received were the hospitality of the household: bread, cheese, oatmeal and a dram of whisky. An important element in the ritual, before any food was touched, was a piece of sheep-hide which was first singed in the fire, put three times with the right hand round the family and then held to the noses of all assembled. This element, the *caisein-uchd*, the breast-stripe, was offered to the goodman of the house by the leader of the boys. The following is a typical rhyme:

> I have come here first
> To renew the Hogmanay;

I need not tell about it,
It was kept in my grandfather's time.
The Calluinn Breast-stripe is in my pocket,
A goodly mist comes from it;
The goodman will get it first,
And shove its nose into the fire upon the hearth.
It will go sunwise round the children,
And particularly the wife will get it;
'Tis his own wife best deserves it,
Hand to distribute the Christmas cakes.
Rise down, young wife,
And young wife who has earned praise;
Rise (and come) down, as you were wont,
And bring down our Calluinn to us.

The cheese, that has the smooth face,
And butter eye has not blinked;
But if you have not that beside you,
bread and flesh will suffice.
There is water in my shoes,
And my fingers are cut,
There is in beside the fire,
What will cure my complaint,
And if you have room to move,
Rise and bring down the glass.

New Year's Day was the Day of Little Christmas, its advent being celebrated by all in the household taking a dram and then a spoonful of half-boiled sowens, the poorest food imaginable, taken for luck. This particular custom was common in the central Highlands but rare in the Western Isles. Salutations of the season were offered. A game of shinty was the order of the day for young boys, as it still is. As for the housewife, she had a long list of rites to perform. Nothing was allowed to be put out of the house on this day, neither ashes, sweepings, dirty water, however useless or however its retention in the house might cause inconvenience. It was a serious matter to give fire out of the house. The first person to enter was an omen of what the new year would bring. The 'first foot' was best if he were a young man bearing a gift of food, drink or fire. Ritual was observed in the byre, with the cattle being sained to protect them from disease and other evils. At the end of the day it was satisfying if the household could review some pleasant hours spent in ensuring that good fortune would come in the ensuing twelvemonth—and in looking forward to another four seasons during which the lore-stock of the community could once again be brought into play to appease the unseen but ever-present spirit world.

CHAPTER 7

Supernatural Beings

HIGHLAND FOLKLORE AND LEGEND is like a shimmering weave of
cloth, shot through with a host of supernatural beings who reflect all
aspects of human fear, endeavour, aspiration, machination, and who
act as agents between the practical earthly planes to which men are
ever physically bound and those accessible only through the exercise of
supernatural powers. Half a hundred of these beings have paraded
before the mind's eye of the Highlander and (who can say?) their real
vision also to establish for themselves a secure niche in the folklore firma-
ment as stars shining with their own characteristic, and occasional
idiosyncratic, brightness. Often they have a cavalier touch of flourish,
flamboyance which sets them apart; others display human characteristics the more to endear them to mortals. These beings are not all,
however, akin to the witches' familiars of times past. Their origins are
too often obscure; in the case of the fairy, their subsequent development into a supernatural society produces a complex organisation,
with rules, taboos and set limits within which its members operated.
Many of the supernatural beings in Highland myth, legend and
folklore are derived from other cultures, notably Norse; echoes from
Ireland and Scandinavia normally resound. The population density of
these beings in Highland folklore is high, which perhaps reflects the
wide range of belief that once existed in the region. Not a few of the
beings have authentic Gaelic derivations and are often associated with
water. A debate could easily be generated based on whether many of
the supernatural beings of the region are the product of fertile imagi-
nations, are personalised human characteristics, or indeed reflect past
cultures and societal structures. The accepted view that all folklore is
valuable as an analytic element in investigations into the bases of exist-
ing societies might well be the starting point to discover where these
supernatural beings come from. Certainly, from the evidence available
in Highland folklore, many of the beings seem to have origins derived
from more practical bases than one would initially suppose. Be that as
it may, the biographical details of the beings in Highland lore are not

only interesting but entertaining and, in one or two cases, provide food for deeper thought.

Bainisg Gaelic: Woman of the Water, or from *eisg*, a satirist. This being is a musical naiad noted for her habit of singing satirical songs. She was rarely seen and then only in the remotest of places by lost wayfarers or herds looking for strayed sheep and cattle.

Bean-nighe This is the nymph who presides over those about to die. Of a very small stature, she was always seen washing their shrouds by the edge of a loch, on the banks of a stream, or at the stepping stones of a ford. While washing the shroud, the *Bean-nighe* sang dirges and bewailed the fate of the doomed. The *Nigheag* is often so absorbed in her washing and singing that she has occasionally been captured. When this mishap occurs she grants her captor three requests on condition of her release. A Gaelic proverb indicates the luck of any captor of a *Bean-nighe*: "The man got the better of the *nigheag* and she gave him his three choice desires." In Perthshire she is described as being small, rotund and clad in a flimsy garment of emerald hue. In Skye, however, she appears as a squat creature, not unlike a small, pitiful child.

One night a handsome young man went to visit his sweetheart at Hougharry, North Uist, and, as was his usual custom, he took all the shortest routes. When he neared his destination he saw a lovely woman whom he did not recognise. Unsure of himself, he turned and took a winding path among the houses in order to avoid her—but however he tried to keep out of her way, she was always in front of him. At last he stopped and she came face to face with him and said: "I know very well where you are going. But it is much better for you to return. The day will not come when you will marry her. Before a year is out you will be drowned, when it is half tide, at Sgeir Rois."

Almost before the final words were out of her mouth, she shrieked and fled to a nearby stream with her shroud. Disturbed, the lad went on his way, sick at heart; but, on thinking the matter over, he assured himself that he need not be afraid—the washer had said he would be drowned at half tide, so why should he not avoid the place at that time? He thought no more about it. A few weeks afterwards, the lad, with three or four others, went to a wedding and, as a short cut, they took to the ford. A sudden mist fell and one of them was lost. It need not be said that at that time it was half tide and the one subsequently drowned at Sgeir Rois was he who had met the *Bean-nighe*.

There are many other tales told about sightings or meetings with the *Bean-nighe*. The most outstanding is that concerning a *Bean-nighe* on the banks of Loch Slin. One Sabbath morning a Cromarty lass was walking along a track skirting the Loch when she saw a strange female figure standing in the water, close by a cluster of rushes. The figure was "knocking claes" on a stone to clean them. On a bleaching-green close by were more than thirty shrouds, all dirty and smeared with blood. The sighting of the apparition was duly reported, but no one could offer any explanation, particularly as not one but many deaths were foretold. Shortly after the appearance of this *Bean-nighe*, the roof of Fearn Abbey collapsed during worship, burying its congregation in debris and killing thirty-six people. Only then, after the shock of the disaster had passed, did the significance of the apparition become clear.

Beithir This was a being with the reputation of being venomous and destructive; it haunted dark caves and mountain corries generally inaccessible to humans. *Beithir* is the Gaelic for lightning and also serpent and the creature's origin is probably derived from an echo of some long-lost belief arising from the destructive character of lightning in high mountainous areas. The serpent association, however, is more interesting as it may reflect a world-wide belief in the serpent as an agent of significant power. In his book *The Dragon and the Disc*, F. W. Holiday presents evidence of serpent culture in the British Isles, as shown, in one particular, in the thousands of rock carvings portraying coils, discs and serpentine figures, both symbolised and real. Legend, too, adds its leaven of water-based creatures with serpentine characteristics ranging from the south of Ireland to Loch Ness, where the popular phenomenon of the 'monster' is not so rare in the British Isles as is commonly supposed.

Blue Men of the Minch The Minch here is that restless stretch of seawater which effectively separates the Outer Hebrides from the west coast of Scotland. The Blue Men of the Minch sport in the narrow tide-way between Lewis and the Shiant Isles (*Seun*: charmed). These creatures are storm-kelpies who give their name to the Gaelic description of this stretch of water: Sruth nam Fear Gorma. Seemingly, it is the function of these kelpies always to keep the waters of their stream as turbulent as possible, so rendering it difficult to navigate. One man who was interviewed by the late Revd John Gregorson Campbell was insistent that he himself had seen one of the Blue Men: "A blue-coloured man, with a long, grey face, and floating from the waist out of the water, followed the boat in which he was for a long time, and was occasionally so near that the observer might have put his hand on him." The Revd Campbell was minister of Tiree from 1861 to 1891 and collected a vast amount of legends and superstitions of the Highlands and Islands.

On some occasions, the skipper of an intercepted boat had to conduct a verbal battle with the Blue Men, answering questions in rhyming couplets. Failure to answer correctly meant his ship being dragged down to the bottom of the Minch.

According to Gaelic tradition, fallen angels were expelled from Heaven in three groups: the fairies to earth; the Blue Men to the sea; and the Nimber Men (*Na Fir Chlis*) banished to the sky to appear as the Merry Dancers.

Bochdan This being was a form-changing creature, able to assume countless forms and shapes, all designed to instil the utmost terror in any human, and that quite successfully. It was encountered as a black dog that accompanied a traveller on part of his way. On other occasions, a headless form appeared. The Bochdan was known for its wide repertoire of noises, varying from clanking chains, moaning, blood-freezing cries and the sounds of throttling. The creature generally was a worthwhile object with which to frighten unruly children and, one suspects, not a few adults besides. The word is from the Gaelic *Bocan*: hobgoblin, sprite, or spectre.

Brownie This creature is akin to the Lare, the hearth-spirit of the Romans. Variously described as being meagre, well-proportioned, shaggy, wild and handsome in his appearance (there are also females of the species), he prefers to haunt the dark corners of large old houses. Thus he tended to be a figure more familiar to the Highland aristocracy and their residential retainers than the more common folk who lived in hypogea or rough huts. He derives his name from his brownish complexion. Though now rare, he was at one time a common adjunct to any family of rank in the Highlands. There are as many stories about the brownie as there are of the fairy, indicating, perhaps, a creature of popular acceptance, if only because of his friendly disposition and willingness to help around the house. His time of activity was during the hours of darkness and after the household had gone to bed. Then he would discharge any laborious task left to him—but not for any reward. So sensitive was this creature that any offer, even of food, as recompense for his labours would drive him away. He was the bane of the household servants. Those who shirked their duties often received a clip on the head from an unseen hand as an encouragement to do better in the future.

The brownie was ubiquitous and was found in big houses in Colonsay, Tiree (where he also acted as herdsman), Castle Lachlan (the home of the MacLachlans), Ardincaple (the MacDougalls), the island of Easdale, with the MacDonalds of Largie in Kintyre, on the island of Gigha, in Glen Moriston, and in the Castle of Invergarry.

Martin Martin (*c.* 1700) had the following tale from Sir Norman

MacLeod about the brownie of Berneray, an island in the Sound of Harris.

Sir Norman had left his island to visit Skye, with no definite time for his return. In his absence his servants and other employees assembled one night in the large hall of his house. One of them, reputed to have been endowed with the second sight, quite unexpectedly informed the assembled company that they ought to quit the hall without delay, since the place would be required later in the evening by another company. His fellow-servants dismissed the suggestion with the observation that there was very little likelihood that Sir Norman and his entourage would return that night, having regard both to the lateness of the hour and to the fact that in the darkness the voyage from Skye was beset with many perils. But the seer maintained his prediction against all argument and reasoning. Within an hour, however, one of Sir Norman's men arrived on the scene, and told the company to provide lights and in other ways prepare the house, since their master had just come ashore in the dark.

When, later, Sir Norman MacLeod was told of this prediction, he sent for the seer, that he might question him personally as to its authenticity. The seer answered that on several occasions during the evening he had observed the brownie enter the hall in human form, and purport to carry to the door an old woman seated by the fire, and that eventually the brownie ejected her by seizing her by the neck and heels. When the seer observed this in the hall he laughed loud and long; but the import of the occurrence was obvious, to him at least, though he was disbelieved by his fellows.

Cailleach-uisge A water-woman, or water-carlin, this being was a supernatural of malign influence frequenting dark caves, woods and carries. She was related to other water-divinities such as the *Bean-nighe, Uraisg, Peallaidh,* all of whom were associated with lochs, streams, rivers and waterfalls. She was the female counterpart of the *Bodach.* Some descriptions use the word *cailleach* to describe the first week in April; she is represented as a wild hag with a venomous temper, hurrying about with a magic wand in her withered hand, switching the grass and keeping down the vegetation, to the detriment of both man and beast. However, when the grass, fed by the warm sun, the dew and the rain, overcomes the *Cailleach,* she flies into a terrible rage and, throwing away her wand into the root of a whin bush, she disappears in a whirling cloud of angry passion until the beginning of April comes again.

Cairbre This is the name of the deity who carried the souls of those slain in battle to *flathanas,* or heaven. Gaelic usage seems to have closely resembled that of other countries in this, as it was customary to place a wax candle, a gold coin, a small hammer, and a pair of scales in the grave with the body. The candle was to light the pilgrim across the dark river of death; the coin to pay the services of the ferryman; the hammer to knock at the door of heaven; and the scales to weigh the soul, which last was done by St Michael, while the chief of the nether regions endeavoured to weigh down his side of the balance. Martin Martin, in his book *A Description of the Western Islands of Scotland*, wrote:

> Between Bernera and the main land of Harris lies the Island of Ensay, which is about two miles in circumference, and for the most part arable ground, which is fruitful in corn and grass; there is an old chapel here, for the use of the natives; and there was lately discovered a grave in the west of the Island in which was found a pair of scales made of brass, and a little hammer, both of which were finely polished.

There are two derivations of the word in Gaelic: *Cairbne*—chariot, ship; *Cairbhe*—corpse.

Caoineag This is a naiad who foretells the death of, and weeps for, those slain in battle. She is sometimes confused with the *Bean-nighe* but cannot be approached or questioned. She is seldom seen, but often heard in hill and glen, in corries, and by lochs and streams. Her mourning causes much alarm to wayfarers and to the relatives of those fighting in war. The sorrowful cry of the *Caoineag* (Gaelic: weeper) was much feared before a foray or a battle. It is said that she was heard for several nights before the Massacre of Glencoe. This aroused the suspicions of the people in the glen and, notwithstanding the assurance of peace and friendship of the soldiery, some people left the Glen and thus escaped the fate of many of those who remained. The following commemorates the occasion:

> Tha caoineag bheag a bhroin
> A taomadh deoir a sula,
> A gil 's a caoidh cor Clann Domhnuill
> Fath mo leoin! nach d'eisd an cumha.

> Little *caoineag* of the sorrow
> Is pouring the tears of her eyes,
> Weeping and wailing the fate of Clan Donald,
> Alas my grief! that ye did not hear her cries.

Ceasg This was a creature of great beauty, half woman, half grilse: a kind of freshwater mermaid. Her main feature was her long, glossy hair. (Gaelic: *Ceasg*—tuft).

Changeling This creature was the bane of every mother of a new-born baby. If certain rituals were not carried out by the midwife at the moment of birth, there was the immediate danger of the fairies appearing to substitute the new-born babe with one of their own ancient senior citizens of the fairy world. The likeness of these ancients to babies was startling and the mother was often unable to detect any trickery until, no matter the amount of care and feeding she gave her supposed child, it never grew. The changeling could be returned to its fairy world only by threatening to cause it some harm or indignity, when the original human child would be brought back.

The changeling represents one of the many features of the close-bound relationship between fairy and mortal, in that the lifestyles of both species contained many common areas which were often interchangeable and that without much friction, with a special "return guaranteed if not satisfied" cause in the unwritten contract. The changeling also highlights a feature of fairy society in that these creatures in time became too old to perform useful functions and had to be cared for. Their imposition of the changeling on human society might indicate a lack of social concern for the elderly on the part of the fairy, rather preferring to shelve responsibility on to others who might be fooled most if not all of the time. The Gaelic word for changeling, *tacharan*, indicates a sprite, an orphan, a weak and helpless being.

Conall This being represents the Celtic Cupid and the guardian spirit of childhood. His protection is always near the little ones whenever they are in danger. A story is told of how a child in Skye was lost in a sudden fall of mist and was benighted in a wild moor in the middle of a storm. But the good *Conall* took the child by the hand and led him to a safe place where he was found by the worried village folk. (Gaelic: *conall*—love, friendship).

Crodh-mara These are sea-cows and are popular in Gaelic folklore. They are described as having red ears, one or both of which are notched. They are probably a traditional echo of the old Caledonian cattle whose ears were also red and which were called *earc iuchd*, or notched cattle. The term *cra-chluasach*, red-eared, was applied to the species of cattle supposedly descended from sea-cows. Calves that came from water-bulls (*tarbh-uisge*) serving ordinary cows are hornless, but what ears there are are red. Martin Martin says: "There are several calves that have a slit in the top of their ears; and these the natives fancy to be the issue of a wild bull that comes from the sea or fresh lakes . . ."

Cu sith This creature is a fairy dog, credited with the ability of exercising the influence of the evil eye. It moves swiftly during the night and is almost certain death to anyone who encounters it. The dogs are large, dark-green in colour and bark three times only within the hearing of an intended victim; there is often an interval between each bark so that the victim has time to look out for himself before he is overtaken and destroyed. The existence in Highland supernatural bestiary of this creature indicates the belief that animals as well as humans populated the spirit world of the Celts. Of the many tales related about the fairy dog, one concerns two men in Benbecula who were spending the night in a hut out on the moors. They were seated before a good fire, talking quietly, when the door burst open and in ran two dogs, leashed together with a cord bespangled with gold and brilliant stones. Both men, and the herded animals in the hut, froze with fright, not knowing what to expect, when a voice from outside called the dogs to heel. The animals rushed outside and the men, with a rare presence of mind, ran after them to see, in the night sky, a host of spirits, the *Sluagh*, with their attendant dogs. These were the spirits of the long departed on a hunting expedition, travelling westwards to Tir fo Thuinn (the Land under Waves). The men heard some of the dogs' names: Slender-fay, Lucky-treasure, and Seek-beyond.

Dealan-de This creature was said to be the Angel of God come to bear the souls of the dead to heaven. If it is seen in or near the house where a person is dead or dying, the omen is good and friends rejoice. If it is not seen, a substitute is made by rapidly twirling a fire-pointed stick, moving it from the dead or dying person towards the door or window. The ancient Egyptians represented the soul leaving the body as a butterfly emerging from the chrysalis, sometimes from the mouth of the dead. The literal meaning of the name in Gaelic is the appearance produced by shaking a burning stick and whirling it around; the word also means lightning or nocturnal brightness in the heavens. The Barra tradition has it that the butterfly a holy creature, perhaps an angel or messenger from heaven and so to kill it was a crime. On that island the following verse is remembered:

> Dealan, dealan, dealan De,
> Beannachd uaim-se go Mac De,
> Is beannachd eile hugad fe.

> Butter, butter, butterfly,
> A blessing from me to the Son of God,
> And another blessing to yourself.

Each uisge This creature is the water-horse, or kelpie, able to assume the forms of men and of women, but favouring that of a handsome, well-groomed horse. It was to be found all over the Highlands and Islands, from populated Perthshire to the remote sheilings of the islands of the Hebrides. Its primary function in the Highland supernatural bestiary was to lure men and women to their deaths in some loch, usually near to a township, and in the depths of which the creature lived. A tradition has it that the *Each-uisge* was an agent in the pay of Satan, commissioned to prosecute the destruction of humans without affording them time to prepare for their immortal interests; he thus endeavoured to send their souls to his master while he was allowed to enjoy the mortal remains. However, the *Each-uisge* had no authority to touch a human of his own free accord, unless the latter was the aggressor. Rather, the *Each-uisge* had to rely on duplicity, presenting himself as some prize: a handsome, well-dressed young man to a young girl, or a fine-looking horse. Using these lures he was given control of the unfortunates who then met their deaths by drowning soon afterwards.

There are probably more tales about the *Each-uisge* than of any other supernatural creature. Many have similar elements and feature the *Each-uisge* in his animal or human form. A tale about the former manifestation concerns a group of children who were playing beside a loch in Sutherland. They were so absorbed in their games that they scarcely noticed a beautiful horse had strayed close to them. One boy, however, saw the animal and, delighted at the chance of riding it, mounted its back. Once up, he called to a playmate to get up behind him, then a third, and a fourth until no fewer than sixteen children were on the horse. But one lad was reluctant to do so and, instead, put his finger on the horse's head, intending only to lead the animal. To his horror, he found he could not remove his finger and he remembered tales at his mother's fireside of the *Each-uisge*. At the same instant, the horse trotted off dragging the boy with him. With great courage, the boy took out a knife and sliced off the top of his finger and freed himself, to see, through his tears of pain and distress, the *Each-uisge* trotting into the waters of the loch with the burden of terrified children.

The *Each-uisge* could, however, be overcome. One man actually tamed one of the species by throwing a bucket of water over the animal every morning and night. One day, however, he told his son to take the horse out for some work, but forgot to ensure that the lad doused the horse with water. This omission from the morning's routine resulted in the lad being dragged to the edge of a nearby loch by the *Each-uisge* which, no doubt pleased with his prize, thought it ample payment for all the free work he had been forced to perform.

One man had an encounter with an *Each-uisge* which gives us an indication of the source of the animal's power. This man, variously named in tradition as MacDonald and MacGregor, met up with an *Each-uisge* and, with a stroke of his sword, cut the animal's bridle so that the bit fell to the ground. This he picked up while the animal recovered from the blow. Little did MacDonald realise that this simple act gave him power over the *Each-uisge*, which he then pestered with questions on the value of the item. It transpired that it was the bridle, a symbol of the animal's Satanic commission, which gave the *Each-uisge* the power of transformation. "Just look through one of the holes of the bit and you will see a number of fairies and witches willing to do your bidding." MacDonald, cautious, preferred to forgo the sight and, after extracting a promise for his own safety, left the *Each-uisge* a sorry animal at having been outwitted by a mortal.

The following tale relates how the last *Each-uisge* in Lewis was killed at Uig, on the west of the island. A man in the parish was tacksman of an extensive tract of land which included a piece of land between Loch Roag and Loch Langavat. In the summer season he used to send his cattle to graze on the moor with two women to look after them; the women lived in a sheiling in Glen Langavat. The women were frequently visited by the *Each-uisge* in human form: a pleasant and agreeable young man whom the women found most attractive. But in time he began to change his attitude towards them, becoming officious, insulting and highly offensive, Matters came to a head when he killed some of the cattle, which sent the women back home with the full tale of what was happening. The tacksman, who did not believe them, was forced, on the insistence of the women, to send two men to investigate the matter. When they arrived at the glen it was in time to see the *Each-uisge*, in his animal form, taking away two of the cattle. Convinced, the tacksman sent for a man who lived in Earshader, on the shores of Loch Roag, who had some renown as a skilled archer, and with the reputation behind him of having killed similar beasts in Skye and another in Lewis. The tacksman offered a reward sufficiently attractive to the archer, who agreed to get rid of the *Each-uisge*. So the archer, named MacLeod, took his bow and arrows and, accompanied by his son, made for Glen Langavat. No sooner had he arrived at the place when the waters of the loch broke to reveal the *Each-uisge*. When the beast came within range MacLeod let off an arrow which hit the creature's side, but did not stop his progress. A second arrow also caught the *Each-uisge*, but only served to enrage it all the more. In desperation, seeing the animal charging towards him and his son, MacLeod took out a special arrow, called *Baobhag*, the Fury of the Quiver, and released it with all the strength he could muster. The sharp point went into the beast's heart and it dropped dead. MacLeod then cut off the tail and took it back to the tacksman as proof, and collected his handsome reward.

Belief in the *Each-uisge* existed until only a few decades ago. In 1840, the Beastie Loch, near Melon Udrigil, Wester Ross, was purged of its supernatural inhabitant. The English proprietor of the estate in which it was situated received a deputation of his tenants who asked that the loch be cleared of the beast, which lay close to a public road. At first the laird refused to believe such a tale, but was finally persuaded to do something. At first pumps were used which, after working for several weeks, only reduced the water level by a few inches. After many other suggestions, it was decided to pour unslaked lime into the deepest part of the loch. So fourteen barrels were taken out into the loch by a small boat, oared by visitors to the district for no native could be found to undertake the task, and dumped overboard. This act seemed to satisfy the laird's tenantry for the *Each-uisge* was never seen again after that—though local tradition had it that the animal merely took itself off to another loch, far from the haunts of interfering men.

Is there a basis for belief in the *Each-uisge*? In 1897, Fr Allan MacDonald, parish priest of Eriskay, took down the following tale from Ewen MacMillen, one of his parishioners:

> Ewen MacMillen, Bunavullin, Eriskay, of Skye descent, aged about fifty, tells me that four years ago at the end of May or the beginning of June, he had gone to look after a mare and foal that he had, about nine or ten o'clock. He went up to Loch Duvat (Black Water) to see them. There was a goodly haze. He passed at the went end a horse belonging to John Campbell, Bunavullin, and a horse belonging to Duncan Beag MacInnes. He saw an animal in front of him at the north side of the lake which he took to be his own mare and was making up to it. He got to within twenty yards of it but could not distinguish the colour on account of the haze but in size it appeared no bigger than a common Eriskay pony. When he came within twenty yards of it the creature gave off a hideous or unearthly scream (*sgiamh grannda*), that terrified not only MacMillen but the horses that were grazing at the west end of the lake, which immediately took fright. MacMillen ran the whole way home and the horses themselves did not stop until they reached home. The horses were not in the habit of coming home, although they might have come home on their own occasionally.

The year 1943 found Lieut Russell Flint in command of a Royal Navy high-speed launch with a crew of twenty on board. As the vessel was travelling down Loch Ness at about 35 knots, a terrific jolt was received by the craft Lieut. Flint records that he saw: "A very large animal form which disappeared in a flurry of water". He had to cable the Admiralty to explain the damaged bows of his craft. Describing the object he hit as "soft and squelchy", one is reminded of a similar description applied to the *Each-uisge* killed in Loch na Mna on Mull

by Alastair na Beisde. After killing the creature he found it to be a
"soft mass" (*sgling*) like a jellyfish. His story is found in J. G. Campbell's *Superstitions of the Highlands and Islands of Scotland* (1900).
F. W. Holiday, in his book *The Dragon and the Disc*, suggests that
the frequent manifestations in the past of water creatures to a
credulous people became absorbed into the lore of their communities;
but the present day has also witnessed similar manifestations in Loch
Ness and Loch Morar, which regularly appear before people who could
not be said to be credulous. Yet the manifestations, Holiday maintains,
have no real basis of existence; he puts the theory that these monsters
are the same type of manifestations as ghosts. Various Loch Ness
witnesses have said that the head of the monster in the Loch is like
that of a goat or sheep. Celtic literature contains references to water-
creatures and describes these as though they were more spiritual than
material: "What fell of monsters by Finn . . . slew the phantom of Loch
Lein, it was a great endeavour to go to subdue it; he slew a phantom in
Druimcliath, a phantom and a serpent in Loch Righ."

The Femori—the legendary invaders of Ireland—were commonly
associated with *goborchinu* (horseheads). Irish legend couples the
Femori with the sea and they were represented as monsters. Sir John
Rhys, the Celtic folklorist, said: "The *goborchinu* or horseheads have
also an interest, not only in connection with the Femori . . . but also as
a link between the Welsh *afanc* and the Highland water-horse."

Fairy Of all the characters and beings in the supernatural world of the
Highlander, the fairy stands closest to him, reflecting his social structure, his life and life-styles, and his occult powers. Perhaps there is
something of the human alter ego in the fairy, as there is inherent in
many other similar spirit types, occupants of the world of supernature. Spirits are symbolic powers invented by man and named by
him as being potent agents in everyday life. They are often endowed
with human characteristics for the very purpose of being able to have
social relationships with them, since this depends upon speech and
mutual exchange. Powers that are not anthropomorphized in this way
remain impersonal, like the magic that can be used by anyone knowing
the correct spell or medicine. When powers are personalised as spirits
they are still essentially nonhuman, elusive and somewhat unpredict-
able. They often receive class names, fairy, elf and the like, rather than
personal names. It is a well-known phenomenon in many societies that
it is dangerous to name a spirit because this is a means of conjuring up
that spirit. Often these spirits are not self-acting, but emerge on the scene
only in response to certain human actions.

Fairies tend to be concerned with local, terrestrial spirits in close
contact with men, and not with the gods whose actions are related to

myth. Fairy stories are rarely heroic tales of high destiny, but rather are about the trials and tribulations of normal life, the luck and misfortune of everyday men and women, despite the occasional use of royal titles. In these stories, the spirits are symbolic devices to account for the accidents that befall man; and the plots concern themselves with the transgressions of some moral rule and the reparations made to overcome these.

The borderline between the human world and fairyland is hazy and tenuous. If it is crossed, then only consistent action can guarantee success in any venture: to err in fairyland results in enchantment.

Fairies have been linked up with the Fates (Latin: *fata*) or birth spirits and hence have a place at christenings. The uninvited fairy, the bad Fate, was always a spirit to be feared, for its presence indicated the possibility of the child being forced to follow an evil destiny in its life career.

Where did the fairies come from? Many differing versions are given to account for their origins. Robert Kirk, Minister of Aberfoyle, who himself was eventually sucked up into fairyland, says they are "of a middle nature betwixt man and Angel, as were daemons thought to be of old". While this definition is not particularly helpful, it can be enlarged upon by reference to other sources, for example *Carmina Gadelica*, a collection of rhymes, spells, incantations and general Gaelic folklore compiled at the end of the nineteenth century by Dr Alexander Carmichael. In the collection there is a rhyme recited by an old man from Barra, who claimed to have heard it when the fairies were dancing and singing by the fairy hill:

> Not of the seed of Adam are we,
> Nor is Abraham our father;
> But of the seed of the Proud Angel
> Driven forth from Heaven.

From the now-deserted island of Mingulay, south of Barra, comes another account:

> The Proud Angel fomented a rebellion among the angels of Heaven where he had been a leading light. He declared that he would go and found a kingdom of his own. When going out at the door of Heaven, the Proud Angel brought "dealanaich dheilgnich agus beithir bheumaich"—prickly lightning and biting lightning—out of the doorstep with his heels. Many angels followed him—so many that at last the Son cried out: "Father! Father! The city is being emptied!", whereupon the Father ordered the gates of Heaven and hell to be closed. Thus, there were spirits who remained in Heaven, while others remained in hell; those who had left Heaven but had

not reached hell flew into the holes of the earth like stormy petrels. These are the fairy folks—ever since doomed to live under the ground, and only permitted to emerge when and where the King permits. They are never allowed abroad on Thursday, that being St Columba's Day, nor on Friday, that being the Son's Day, nor on Saturday, that being Mary's Day, nor on Sunday, that being the Lord's Day. On certain nights when their bruthain or bowers are open, and their lamps lit, and the song and the dance are moving merrily, the fairies may be heard singing.

The Revd Robert Kirk reported that fairies have "light changeable bodies, somewhat of the nature of a condens'd cloud, and best seen in twilight", the time of the day, incidentally, Kirk himself joined the fairy flock. "These bodies", he continues, "be so pliable, through the subtilty of the spirits that agitate them, that they can make them appear or disappear at pleasure." Elsewhere in his treatise *Secret Commonwealth of Elves, Fauns and Fairies* (1692), Kirk speaks of their bodies as being of "congealed air . . . which when divides unites again". Obviously bodies of congealed air or condensed cloud are clearly bound to set no small problem in dietetics, but Kirk further reports that:

> some have bodies or vehicles so spungious, thin and desecate, that they are fed only by sucking into some fine spirituous liquors, that pierce like pure air and oyl; others feed more gross on the foyson or substances of cornes and liquors, or on corne itself, that grows on the surface of the earth, which these fairies steall away, partly invisible, partly praying on the grain as do Crows and Mice.

There are many hints at the special relationship that existed between the fairies and mankind in the Highlands and Islands, since fairies have often become the companions of individual human beings. This fairy-human relationship is a complex one, but is also a fascinating aspect of fairy belief. Kirk mentions that in some parts of the Highlands it was believed that the souls of their ancestors dwelt in fairy hills; though Kirk himself adhered to the other and older view that the fairies were a race apart: "the middle order".

The life-style of the fairy realm was startlingly similar to that of their human neighbours above ground, as was their speech and clothing, their fondness for pleasure, and their predilection for quarrelling, "Envy, Spite, Hypocrasy, Lying and Dissimulatione"; though they were not given to swearing or intemperance. The closeness of the fairy to mankind is given in the many fairy associations of plants and topographical features, indicating the manner in which the fairy dominated the minds of the people:

Breaca-sith—Fairy marks which were livid spots appearing on the face of the dead or dying.

Marcachd shith—Fairy riding, which was a paralysis of the spine in animals, alleged to be brought on by the fairy mouse riding across the backs of the animals while they lay on the ground.

Piob shith—The fairy pipe, or elfin pipe, generally found in underground houses.

Miaran na mna sithe—The thimble of the fairy woman: the foxglove.

Lion na mna sithe—The lint of the fairy woman; this is fairy flax said to be beneficial for certain illnesses.

Curachan na mna sithe—oracle of the fairy woman, which is the shell of the blue valilla.

In placenames the element *sith* is common, as in Gleann-sith (Glenshee) in Perthshire; Sithean a Bhealaich, the fairy knoll of the pass at Benmore in South Uist; Beinn Shidhe (Benside), a crafting township near Stornoway, Lewis.

The Highland fairy had a strong predilection for babies. Even as late as the turn of this century, babies in Lewis were watched carefully until they had been baptised. In the event of the mother having to leave her baby unguarded in a room, it was the custom to lay the fire tongs in the doorway or, more generally, across the cradle. Failure to do so resulted in the consequences which feature in many stories, the exchange of the child for a changeling. The fairies never abducted a child without leaving something in its stead—so much to their credit and perhaps an indication of their rather twisted sense of morality. However, the substitute left was usually extremely meagre and emaciated, having a cadaverous appearance and with a tone of voice more like that of an old person than a child. There was the belief that the substitute was a worn-out, decrepit fairy, whom age and disease had rendered an unfit member of the fairy community, and was metamorphosed into a baby.

In Pabbay, an island in Loch Roag, Lewis, a child of a few days was kidnapped by fairies as the result of the carelessness of a woman who had been left in charge of the child. At first the parents did not suspect that it was not their own child they were rearing until an old woman from Valtos, the village opposite the island and on the Lewis mainland, came across for a visit. She commented on the child's appearance and, on a closer look, the parents realised that indeed they had a fairy changeling on their hands. Their problem was then how to get their own child back. The old woman advised them to leave the changeling one midnight on the side of a hillock in the neighbourhood and not to trouble themselves about it until morning at dawn, when they should go to the same place and find their own child. This the parents did and were overjoyed to get their baby returned to them. In time the child grew up and died at a good old age; she was always pointed out in the locality as the one who returned from the fairies.

In a now-deserted village in Uig, Lewis, called Erista, a man had his child stolen by the fairies—who, of course, left a changeling in its place, a sick and unhealthy being which did not deserve the tender care bestowed on it by the man and his wife. Slowly it became apparent to the parents that what they had was not their own child and with some fear for the future they went to visit a local woman known to be wise in these matters. There was, however, some doubt in the parents' minds that the changeling was their own child. There was only one way to find out, they were told by the woman: the wife was to knead a bannock of meal and to bake it against the fire, supported on nine wooden pegs or pins—the lower ends had to be fixed in the hearth, and the others stuck in the edge of the bannock. The instructions were followed to the letter and the wife hid close by to see what would happen. The wife was not long concealed when she saw the child in the cradle raise its head and, after looking round, heard it exclaim: "S fada beo mi, ach chan fhaca mi a leithid do chul-leac ri bonnach" (I have lived long, but I never saw such a back stone (support) to a bannock.) When the mother heard a child of its supposed age speak in such accents and tones of an old man she realised that indeed she had been nursing a changeling. She consulted with the local wise woman again, who advised her to take the changeling to the side of a burn and make as if to throw it into the water. She did this and was subjected to long and piteous appeals for mercy, which she ignored and left the changeling on the bank. The following morning she found her own child sleeping peacefully in the cradle which the day before had been occupied by the redundant fairy.

Highland fairies were usually of a gentle nature, though mischievous. Some types were otherwise. The story is told of the experience of three men, the nub of which was a notion once prevalent among the folk of the region that it was imprudent to wish—or rather express a wish—for anything at any time of the night without simultaneously invoking the protection of the deity. If this invocation were forgotten or neglected, the wish would be granted in some terrible way. Three men went hunting among the hills of Kintail. They had, however, little success and were reluctant to return home empty-handed. They decided therefore to pass the night in a moor hut. They lit a fire, cooked some venison and made themselves comfortable on some dry grass and moss. Two of them sat on one side of the fire while the third, on the other side played a trump (jew's harp). One of the pair began to talk of their unsuccessful day's toil and wished that they had their sweethearts with them in the sheiling.

Almost immediately, the door of the hut opened and three women entered, each pairing herself off with one man. By this time the fire had burned itself to a low dimness, but produced sufficient light for the musician to see, much to his horror, a stream of blood flowing towards the hearth stones. At the same time he was able to see that the feet of the woman who sat by him were like those of a deer. In terror he rose and dashed out of the hut, with his erstwhile companion tearing after him like the wind. He ran all the faster, fear adding a considerable distance to each step he took, and it was only his physical fitness that managed to get him to the door of the nearest human dwelling— but not before he heard the woman saying, with words that floated to him in the night air: "Dhith sibhs'ur cuthaich fein ach dh'fhag mo cuthaich fein mise!" (You ate your own victims but mine escaped from me.)

On the following day the musician with some other men went to the hut where they found, badly mangled, the bodies of his two companions. He was at a loss to understand the whole business until an old man said that the women who had visited them were none other than the *Baobhan sith*, the fairy furies.

The following are typical of fairy stories once told by the fireside throughout the region; they are in fact tales which were in circulation in the Hebrides about the turn of this century.

In the village of Mangersta, Lewis, there was an important person in the community who was always pointed out as being a fairy. He was about thirty years old at the time a visitor to the village was told about him—yet the person was as powerless as an infant of a few days. He was quite incapable of changing the position in which he was placed in bed; he could not extend his hand to his mouth and was unable to eat food properly. He was, in fact, a walking skeleton and looked very much older than his supposed years. He was deaf but not dumb. The story was that as a child he was plump and healthy before he changed almost overnight to the poor specimen that now walked the village. Though they did not say it aloud, the villagers knew in their own minds that he was in fact a fairy changeling.

In an island in Loch Roag, Lewis, there is a conical hillock said to have been a frequent resort of fairies. The day came when some crofters decided to build a turf wall to prevent cattle from straying on to the arable land. The line of the wall passed close to the base of a hillock and, for convenience, the men cut a quantity of turf from it. The following day, a young lad, who was an amateur bagpipe player, sat near the hillock and was cutting a piece of wood for a chanter when he heard a strange sound. Turning round he saw a small woman who told him that she could put him in the way of getting a much better chanter than he could make himself. On asking what she meant, the woman said that she would see to it provided that all the sods cut from the hillock were replaced. The lad then set to and just as he had finished his task the woman appeared again. After expressing thanks for his co-operation, she told him to get *maidne nan cuaran*—a stick stuck in the walls of old houses and on which brogues were hung— and work it down to the shape of a chanter, to bore it carefully and then to insert into it a reed which she handed over to him. This he did and the music that he played on the pipes afterwards excelled the best of any piper in Lewis. This chanter was kept for many generations by the descendants of the land and it went with them when they emigrated to America.

On a hill called Beinn Bhreac, local folk frequently saw a fairy milking deer. She was seen one day by two hunters who were on the hill after deer. The fairy was observed to gather a herd of the animals in a small gorge and then proceed to milk them while she sang a kind of lullaby. One deer ran away and, on seeing this, she followed with almost equal speed; but she lost ground and resorted instead to magic by saying:

> Finlay's arrow in thee, thou thief,
> In spite of thy hoofs it will make thee stop;
> Mac Iain Chaoil's lead in thy carcass
> And the fairy's buarach on thy horns [legs].

The reference to Finlay is Finlay, Chief of the Fairies, evident from the race being frequently called *Sluagh Fhionnlaidh*, or Finlay's People. A buarach is a kind of shackle made of hair or hemp used to tie round the hind legs of cows to keep them from kicking while they were being milked, a device used universally in the Hebrides.

No sooner had the fairy woman uttered the above words than the deer stopped running and allowed herself to be milked. This particular fairy is celebrated in the pibroch of *Cronan Cailleach na Beinne Bric*, which has an air which imitates the tones and modulations in her voice as was heard in the lullaby she used while milking the deer.

A man from Harris was one day hunting in Bealach a' Sgail in North Uist when he came across another man in the act of skinning a deer. The man, who appeared to be a stranger, seemed to be greatly disconcerted at being thus caught and expressed the hope that he had fallen into sympathetic hands. The Harris man assured him that he had nothing to fear on his account. Encouraged by this, the stranger talked further and asked if he had a dog. Replying in the negative, the Harris man was surprised when the stranger offered his own dog, a grizzled hound. Overcome by the generous gesture, the Harris man stooped to catch the dog's leash and turned round to thank the stranger. To his great surprise, and fear, neither the stranger nor the deer carcass was to be seen. But the dog was real enough and stayed with the Harris man for a long time . . . until one day when both were passing a hillock. A shrill whistle was heard, the dog cocked its ears and made off and was never seen again.

In the island of Bernera, Lewis, there is a small hillock called Sit-hean, with a local tale attached to it. A man in the village had a house close by the hillock and was continually annoyed by the fairies who made a habit of borrowing pots and cooking-pans from his wife, sometimes returning them and sometimes not. One day the crofter arrived home from fishing, hungry for a bite to eat, and asked for something hot to be made ready. In reply, his wife said that as the fairies had taken away the pot that morning she could do nothing until it was returned. This was not good enough and he told her to get along to a neighbour and borrow a pot from her. The wife did as she was told and, on the way, passed the hillock. To her surprise there was a door in it and, directly opposite, her own pot. In she went and saw a number of small people sitting about, including an old man wearing a green cap. A large dog was nearby, leashed to a yellow collar. No sooner had she picked up the pot when the old man ordered the dog to be un-leashed and sent after the woman. But the good wife had a good turn of speed in her heels and managed to evade the chasing dog. She had just reached her own doorway when the dog caught her foot with its teeth, but, despite a struggle, she made the safety of her house. The woman had in fact incurred the wrath of the fairies by not reciting the accepted formula which had always to be said by the lender on hand-ing over an article to a borrower: "A blacksmith is entitled to coal to grind the cold iron; a kettle is entitled to a bone and to be sent home safely." These lines ensured that the pot was always returned, never empty but with meat in it.

Stories about fairies, containing elements of reality, are still related. One evening, as darkness fell, a little boy, some eighty years ago, was waiting for the return of his mother from a visit to an ailing neigh-bour. He and his elder sister had been left with their grandmother while their mother was on her errand of mercy. Another little boy joined the two children and the three played happily until it was time to go home. As the distance was too far for the little ones to travel by themselves an elderly woman from the village, visiting their grand-mother, said she would accompany them home. As they went along, the woman said that she would show them something to interest them. Down by the path close to a burn they went and then stopped. "Look, do you see them?" the old lady asked the children. On a hillside, as the children looked, fairies dressed in green danced in a ring round a fire. The children were excited and told their story when they arrived home. Mrs Mona Smith of Edinburgh, the wife of a minister, was the daughter of the little boy in the story. Her family never tired of hearing the tale, corroborated by an aunt from Skye, and always went to visit the green, grassy mound "where Papa saw the fairies". A number of years ago Katharine M. Briggs, the English folklorist who has researched extensively into the realm of fairy records, said that she met the little boy when he was an old man; but not so old that he could not recall all the details of that evening in the Skye gloaming. An important element in this modern fairy tale is that the woman who showed the children the fairies was credited with the gift of second sight; through her gift, seemingly, the fairies were seen by the children.

Another fairy experience concerns a man, still living, who, while a child in the Hebrides, had a series of visions with lights and music and conflicts between good and evil fairies. Part of the experience was full of delight and blessing, but part was also terrifying and painful from the dreadful cries that drowned the music and the waves of darkness that came over the light. As in the previous instance, an island woman came to his rescue with comfort by explaining that the cries of anguish which he had heard were those of the evil fairies who were prevented from harming him and were angry that the good fairies should have anything to do with him. This account is similar to one of Robert Kirk who said of men with second sight: "And glaid would he be to be quit of such, for the hideous Spectacles seen among them; as the torturing of some Wight, earnest ghostly stairing Looks, Skirmishes, and the like."

Another story comes from Islay, told by the Postmaster at Portnahaven to Miss Elspeth Stirling. It concerns a malevolent fairy. A brother and sister were walking along a road near to a loch when a little man ran past them, touching the boy as he passed. The boy was paralysed for the rest of his life. His little sister, who was wearing green, was uninjured. Paralysis has always been thought to be a fairy evil; green, too, was a dangerous colour to wear, though in this instance it seems to have been a safeguard from injury.

Osgood MacKenzie, in his book *A Hundred Years in the Highlands*, tells of an unusual nature fairy called the *Ghillie Dhu*. He haunted birch woods, dressed in leaves and moss. MacKenzie relates how a little girl called Jessie Macrae got lost in the woods one summer night. But she was found by the fairy who treated her well and took her safely to a path which brought her to her home again, which was at Loch a Druing, in Gairloch, Wester Ross. The *Ghillie Dhu* was so named from the colour of his black hair; he was seen by many people during a period of more than forty years in the latter half of the eighteenth century. So strong was the belief in this being that soon afterwards, no fewer than five lairds made a hunting trip into the woods to shoot the *Ghillie Dhu*. Needless to say the creature was not seen after little Jessie's experience; perhaps the intent of the hunting party was scented and the *Ghillie Dhu* decided that discretion was the better part of valour and faded from mortal ken.

Fath-fith This is a term applied to the occult power which rendered a person invisible to mortal eyes and which could transform one object into another. Men and women were made invisible; or men were transformed into bulls, horses or stags, while women changed into cats, hares or hinds. The Fath-fith was especially useful to hunters, warriors and travellers, rendering them invisible or unrecognisable to enemies and to animals. The transmutations were either voluntary or involuntary.

One of the most popular tales in Celtic mythology is that of Fionn and his son Ossian. Fionn had a fairy sweetheart, but he left her to marry a human wife. The fairy, with a natural resentment of the slighting, placed his new wife under a Fath-fith spell and changed her into the form of a hind of the hill. In time Fionn's wife gave birth to a son and, as would a hind, she licked the baby's forehead when he was born. The result was that hair grew on that part of the child's temple and he became known as Ossian, the fawn. In time the boy grew up to reach the years when he must learn to hunt. One day he came on a green corrie and saw a timid hind. The chase instinct was strong and he drew back his spear to kill the animal, when the hind spoke to him and said that she was his mother in a hind's form. Startled but convinced, Ossian went with his mother into a rock-cave where he was entertained by the hind who changed into a tall, beautiful woman. After three days or so, Ossian thought, he returned to the mortal world to find that in fact he had been absent for three years. Impressed by his experience, he composed the well-known Gaelic poem 'Sanas Oisein d'a Mhathair' (Ossian's Warning to his Mother), of which at least fourteen versions exist today.

Fuath In Gaelic this word means hatred, aversion and a hateful object, from which it can be assumed that the *Fuath*, as personalised by folklore, was a spectre, demon or apparition able to strike fear into the eye and heart of the beholder. Occasionally the *Fuath* is associated with water, to become a water-beast or kelpie. It frequented glens, rivers and waterfalls. The spectre has different attributes in different tales.

Frid Highland people apply the term *frid* and its derivatives (*fridean, frideag,* and *fridich*) to creatures which were supposed to live in the internal rocks and in the innermost parts of the earth. It was said that these gnomes ate and drank like men and so it was not right that they should be deprived of the crumbs that fell to the ground, nor any drops of milk that fell to the floor. Old people used to deprecate the removal of these morsels by saying: "*Gabh ealla ris, is ioma bial feumach tha feitheamh air.*" (Let it be; many are the needy mouths awaiting it.)

Glen Liadail in South Uist was supposed to be peopled by the *Frid* who, while friendly to the humans living in the glen, were resentful of strangers. It was necessary for any wayfarer to sing a propitiatory song before entering the glen. On one occasion the wife of a crofter in an adjoining glen was left alone with her child when she felt the house becoming oppressively full of people. She knew that these were the *Fridich*, who went about in great clouds, like midges, but who were invisible to mortal eyes. The woman was afraid, but retained her presence of mind and sang an extempore song in which she highly praised the gnomes. They, being intensely sensitive to flattery, did no harm to the lonely woman and her child; before the song was ended, they had left the house as silently as they had come. Gaelic: *Frid*—gnome, pigmy, elf, rock-elfin.

Gainisg This being is a minor deity which lives among reeds and marshes on the borders of lochs and the banks of rivers. Its main function seems to be the presaging of deaths by moaning and wailing, particularly before storms. *Gainisg* in Gaelic is the common-sedge, the long coarse grass among which this naiad weeps and moans.

Glaistig This creature is an amphibious sprite. Half-woman, half-goat, the *Glaistig* frequents lonely lochs and rivers. She was a tutelary being, thin, grey in appearance and with long yellow hair; she was often clothed in green. She tended to be a natural solitary and was never seen in more than pairs. Her main duty was tending cattle and offering help around the fold. For this work she received a libation of fresh milk placed in a large basin-stone. She was also associated with herding deer. She occupied a middle position between the fairies and mankind. She was, however, not a fairy woman, but supposed to be one of the human race who had a fairy nature in her. The derivation of her name is from *glas* (water) and *stic* (imp).

As a general rule the *Glaistig* was harmless to humans and at times she appeared almost loveable, particularly in tales of old vintage. In later tales, however, the *Glaistig* appears as an irritable creature. In one story an attempt is actually made on a man's life. The *Glaistig* is credited with a particular love for children, especially in earlier tales.

Some stories relate the times when the women of a Highland township would milk their cattle in the shelling while the *Glaistig* would play hide and seek with their little ones behind stones and bushes. But as her existence lengthened her years, the *Glaistig*'s character changed.

From the loveable creature of tradition, she degenerated into a kind of female ruffian. Instead of reciting rhymes to the children, she threw insults. Instead of offering her help around the sheilings, she threw stones at humans and caused no end of bother. The background of the *Glaistig* is one of gradual rejection of her former habits; old age did not come alone. But . . . perhaps it is more the character of the Highlands which changed rather than the *Glaistig*?

There are many tales about the *Glaistig*, or rather certain of her species, for she and her like were well spread throughout the region. One *Glaistig* is credited with an attempt to build a bridge across the Sound of Mull. This creature gathered a huge creelful of stones from the hills of North Morvern and walked down to the Sound with her burden. However, her creel-strap broke and the stones fell scattered to the ground, and she gave up in disgust. The stones are still there for anyone to see, lying in a heap known as Carn-na-Caillich.

In some tales the *Glaistig* is associated with the famous Highland freebooters, Gilleasbuig MacIain Ghiorr and his brother Ranald. She would invariably find her way to their haunts after a successful raid to ask for her share of the spoils. When asked how she knew where to find them, she replied: "Bha mi air Sgurr Eige" (I was on the Sgurr of Eigg), a phrase which is still often used as a proverb in the Western Isles, to indicate a position with a bird's-eye view. Once the pirate brothers flattered themselves on evading the *Glaistig*. This was when they invaded Barra to make good a threat they had thrown out to the MacNeill Chief. But that night, as they sat by the fire, the *Glaistig* appeared to demand her share of the loot.

A *Glaistig* forsook the township of Ach-na-Creige in Mull because of the trickery of a herd-boy. In the township cattle-fold, there was a large stone with a round hole in it, into which was poured some of the evening's milking. In return for this libation, the *Glaistig* would watch the cattle overnight. One evening a herd-boy poured boiling milk and went into hiding to watch the proceedings. The poor creature burnt her tongue so much that she promptly deserted her duties and the cattle of that township were never again watched over.

The *Glaistig* had a love for mischief which sometimes rebounded on herself. She had to leave the district of Glenborrodale in Skye because of her annoying tricks. In the district there was a blacksmith whom she loved to tease and bother on every available occasion. The smith tolerated the *Glaistig* for a long time until she took to hammering away on his anvil in the middle of the night. So he crept into the smithy, took firm hold of the *Glaistig*'s familiar, her *Isean*, a small imp, and made to thrust its hand into the fire. Terror seized the *Glaistig* and she swore to stop her pranks. Though her pride was hurt, she kept her promise and was never seen after that night.

One night Big Kennedy of Lianachan in Lochaber, MacAualrig Mor, was returning home when he crossed the path of a *Glaistig*. He caught her and put her on his saddle in front of him with his sword-belt round her waist. When he got home he locked her in an outhouse. In the morning he heated the coueter of his plough, fetched the *Glaistig* from her night's imprisonment and forced her to swear to never again molest any man or woman in the district, while the sun shone by day or the moon by night. The *Glaistig*, only too willing to comply, stretched out her hand and touched the coulter, only to receive a bad burn. In a shriek of agony she flew into the air and pronounced a curse on Big Kennedy and his seed for all time.

Gobhar bacach This creature was a lame goat and was regarded as an ill omen. It travelled the countryside and lay down on the best land. Several places in the Highlands are known to have been spots having been laid on by the beast. It was once held as a sign that a particular croft or farm is a good one.

Gruagach This is a female spectre of the class of brownies' to which Highland dairymaids made frequent libations of fresh milk. She frisked and gambolled about the cattle pens and folds, armed only with a pliable reed, with which she switched all who annoyed her by uttering obscene language, or by neglecting to leave for her a share of the dairy produce. In Gaelic, *gruagach* is a word meaning wizard-champion and is, strangely, masculine. Her main duty was to preside over cattle and take an intense interest in all matters pertaining to them. In return for her supervision she was offered a libation of milk each evening after the cows were milked. If the libation were omitted, the cattle, notwithstanding all precautions, would all be found broken loose and trampling the corn. If the omission were persisted in, the best cow in the fold would be found dead. The libation was usually poured on to a special stone, the *Clach na Gruagaich*. At one time there was hardly a district in the region which did not have a flagstone on which milk was regularly poured. Nearly all of these stones are erratic ice blocks, with slight cavities. A rune was chanted while the milk was being poured

A woman from the island of Heisgeir, off North Uist, once gave a graphic description of a *Gruagach*: she was seen moving about in the silver light of the moon, with a tall conical hat, with rich golden hair falling about her shoulders like a mantle of shimmering gold, while, with a slight swish of her wand, she would gracefully turn on her heel to admonish an unseen cow. At intervals her mellow voice could be heard in snatches of eerie song as she moved about the grassy ruins of the old nunnery.

It is reported in the *New Statistical Account for Scotland*, dealing with the Parish of Kilmuir, in Skye (1842):

Some time ago the natives firmly believed in the existence of the Gruagach, a female spectre of the class of Brownies, to whom the dairy-maids made frequent libations of milk. The Gruagach was said to be an innocent supernatural visitor . . . Even so late as 1770, the dairy-maids, who attended a herd of cattle in the island of Trodda, were in the habit of pouring daily a quantity of milk in a hollow stone for the Gruagach. Should they neglect to do so they were sure of feeling the effects of the Brownie the next day. It is said that the Rev Donald MacQueen, the then minister of this Parish went purposely to Trodda to check that gross superstition. He might then have succeeded for a time in doing so, but it is known that many believed in the Gruagach's existence long after that reverend gentleman's death.

The following account of a *Gruagach* is dated 1895 and concerns a *Gruagach* who frequented West Bennan in Arran. The creature lived in a cave known as Uamh na Gruagaich, and sometimes Uamh na Beiste, the cave of the monster. She herded the cattle in the township of Bennan and no spring loss, no death loss, no mishap of disease ever befell them, while they throve, fattened and multiplied. Often the *Gruagach* was seen in the bright sunshine, golden hair streaming in the morning breeze and her rich voice filling the air with melody. She would wait on a hillock until the cattle arrived for her supervision.

The *Gruagach* seems to have been part of the fairy structure, though in recent times there are indications that she was given a more ghostly character. In older times, however, she was certainly closely related to the fairy. Thus the creature has affinities with the banshee, the brownie and the ghost. Otta Swire, in her book *The Outer Hebrides and Their Legends*, says:

> In Old Gaelic 'Gruagach' meant a young chief, or more literally 'the long-haired one'; later it came to be used of a spirit, and in some districts [in Skye], a long-haired youth in a fine white shirt (often frilled) and knee breeches; but more frequently in Skye the Gruagach was a very tall thin woman with hair falling to her feet; she wore a soft misty robe, the effect being described as like 'a white reflection or shade'. She was usually the former mistress of the house or land she haunted, who had either died in childbirth or been put under enchantment. She belonged to the site and not to the occupant, and she was seldom seen unless something was about to happen to that site. She helped the owners by caring for cattle and small children (so long as they allowed no dog near her) and the simple were also under her protection. Like the English Brownie, she was partial to a dish of cream. She could sometimes be seen weeping or showing great joy. This reflected joy or sorrow about to fall on the house or land she served. In her character of former mistress of the house or land she haunted, the Gruagach

takes on ghostly connotations. However, in her care of cattle and small children we see an indication of her original function.

Loireag This creature is a water sprite who presided over cloth-making activities: warping, weaving, waulking and the washing of webs of cloth. If the village women omitted any of the traditional usages and ceremonies of these occasions she would resent their neglect in various ways. If a song was inadvertently sung twice at a waulking, the *Loireag* would make the web as thin as before, to render all the work of the woman to no avail. If a woman sang out of tune, the *Loireag* became really angry. A libation of milk was usually given as reward to the *Loireag* for her oversight of the processes. But if this were denied her she would suck the goats, sheep and cows of the townland and place a spell on them so that they could not move.

The following story is from Benbecula: Benmore was always eerie because of the *Loireag* living there. She is a small mite of womanhood, who does not belong to this world, but to the world beyond. She used to drive the people in Benmore distracted, but there is now no one there except the sheep. She is a plaintive little thing, but stubborn and cunning. There was once a little cross carle in Benmore and the *Loireag* was sucking his cow. His daughter tried to drive her away but she could not. So she went in and told her father that neither the *Loireag* nor the cow would heed her. The little carle leapt out at the door in a red rage. He threw a boulder at the *Loireag*, but struck the cow instead and nearly killed her. He then seized the point of the cow's horn in the name of St Columba, and immediately the cow leaped away from the *Loireag*. The latter then ran away into the distance.

In Gaelic, *loireag* means handsome; or a rough and shaggy cow.

Luch-sith This creature is a fairy mouse and is part of the fairy realm. In a more practical world it might be seen as the lesser shrew, an animal which was much disliked because it was believed it caused paralysis of the spine in sheep, cows and horses, simply by running across the animal while it lay down. This disease is called *marcachd shith*, the fairy riding. In some districts the term was applied to the perspiration, due to weakness, which comes out on cattle. The diminutive size of the *Luch-sith*, and its mode of travelling under a grass sward, no doubt made it a favourite candidate for fairy associations.

Luideag The character of this creature is derived from the Gaelic word meaning ragged and slovenly. The being is mostly associated with Skye, particularly near a small loch between Broadford and Sleat known as Lochan nan Dubh Breac, the loch of the black trout. The creature was seen towards the middle of last century in her usual dishevelled state in the neighbourhood of the nearby public road. She never answered when spoken to and often disappeared as mysteriously as she appeared. She finally disappeared for good when a man was found dead, lying by the roadside close to her favourite haunting place.

Merfolk These creatures are the seawater equivalents of the freshwater land-based beings of Highland lore and tradition. The central figure of the species is the mermaid; the male counterpart is often less featured in tales. Ever since recorded history, and before that in oral tradition, the human species has given its imagination a fair easing of the leash to conjure up many fantastic creatures, some quite outrageous. But many animals of the 'fantastic' kind eventually proved their existence —such as the gorilla, frighteningly described by explorers from the seventeenth century but dismissed as figments of a fertile imagination, until it was discovered in 1840. Sea serpents and sea monsters have also been subjected to disbelief until proof was obtained with carcasses of giant squids and the like.

The merfolk are half-human, half-fish. The voice and language are articulate and human. William Munro, a schoolmaster of Thurso, and Hugh Miller, the famous Cromarty geologist, both gave voice to their belief in the creature; neither was in any doubt that the creature he had seen was a mermaid. There is, sadly, no room here to relate their accounts, nor the dispositions by a farmer and girl solemnly recorded in 1811 by the Sheriff-Substitute of Campbeltown, in the presence of the parish minister.

Typical of the stories concerning mermaids is that relating an encounter at close quarters on Benbecula. Some time about 1830 the islanders were cutting seaweed for fertiliser on the shore when one of the women went to wash her feet at the lower end of a reef. The sea was calm and a splash made her look up and out to seaward. What she saw caused her to cry out The rest of the party, hurrying to her, were astonished by the sight of a creature "in the form of a woman in miniature", some few feet away in the sea.

The little sea-maiden, unperturbed by her audience, played happily, turning somersaults and otherwise disporting herself. Several of the men waded out into the water and tried to capture her. But she swam easily beyond their reach. Then a wretched little boy threw stones at her; all missed except one which caught her in the back. At that reception the creature went from the sight of the amazed party.

She was heard of a few days later; but by then she was dead. Her body was washed ashore, about two miles from where she was first seen. A detailed examination followed and we learn that "the upper part of the creature was about the size of a well-fed child of three or four years of age, with an abnormally developed breast. The hair was long, dark and glossy, while the skin was white, soft and tender. The lower part of the body was like a salmon, but without scales."

The lifeless body of the little mermaid attracted crowds to the beach where she lay, and the island spectators were convinced that they had gazed on a mermaid at last. Mr Duncan Shaw, Factor for Clanranald, a baron-baillie and sheriff for the district, after seeing the corpse, gave orders that a coffin and shroud be made for the mermaid and, in the presence of many people, she was buried a little distance above the shore where she was found. It is said that the Factor, being hardly as credulous as his tenants, ordered a coffin and shroud to indicate that the creature was, in his mind at least, partly human in character.

The late Calum I. MacLean, of the School of Scottish Studies, told a meeting of the British Association in Glasgow in 1958 that an old fisherman of the Hebridean island of Muck averred that in 1947 he saw a mermaid, sitting among his lobster-boxes and combing her hair. She dived back into the sea when she realised she was being watched. No amount of questioning, said Mr MacLean, could shake the old fisherman's conviction that he had seen a mermaid.

Some families in the north and west of Scotland claim descent from the merfolk, generations before. One family at Fearn, Ross-shire, numbered a mermaid among their ancestors. Another family at nearby Tarbet believed no member of their relations could ever be drowned, owing to a promise made by a mermaid to one of their kin in the past. The Clan MacLaren have a tradition that they, too, are descended from the union between a man and a mermaid.

One rather touching legend concerns the pebbles known as The Mermaid's Tears, found on the shore at Iona. The story tells of a mermaid who fell in love with one of the brothers of the community; the latter was similarly affected and prayed earnestly that she might be endowed with a human heart, human speech, and a soul which could be saved. But the mermaid, realising the inevitability of her state of life and living, had to keep to her life in the sea. But as often as she could, she came ashore to meet her lover and to shed the tears which became petrified as they fell to the shore.

Peallaidh This was a mysterious being with long untidy hair who haunted streams. It does not seem to be especially uncanny nor to have had an interfering disposition; very little is known about it. At least one of the favourite spots of the species is now called after it: Aberfeldy, which in Gaelic is *Aber Pheallaidh*, the confluence of the *Peallaidh*. From the ragged, untidy appearance of this spirit come the words *peallach*, *peallag*, and *pealtag*.

Seals Though the seal is far from being a supernatural creature, the fact that it has an association in Highland folklore with the supernatural justifies its place in this chapter. The belief that seals are in reality human beings under a deep spell of enchantment has been rooted in folklore and tradition for many centuries. The origin of the belief has now become so diffused that it is extremely difficult to say where the essence of truth lies; for all tales and legends are not the product of pure fancy and fantasy. One story says that a Lewisman named MacCodrum once killed a cuckoo in a hawthorn bush. This deed so angered the fairies, who regard the bird as part of their own world, that they laid a curse on the poor man and his clan: for nine days and eight nights they should retain their seal form, but on the ninth night they should shed their seal skins and become human beings once more, and so on for ever. Others say that the MacCodrums can take human form for the three nights of each full moon. This tale is a layer over an older tradition that the Clan MacCodrum, particularly of North Uist, are derived from sealfolk; but so are other clans. In the Hebrides, as in the northern isles of Orkney and Shetland, there is a finely carved corpus of lore, stirring tales and ballads which revolve around the relationships between seal and human.

The belief in the human origins of seals is extensive and not al all confined to the Highlands and Islands of Scotland. In Scandinavia, the Baltic countries, in Ireland, Iceland, Greenland and Alaska there are tales of wonder in the relationship between men and sea-creatures. In Scotland the culmination of the belief, serving a grand and typical example of the genre, is the Scottish ballad 'The Great Silkie of Skule Skerry'. In Scottish and Irish folklore, however, the belief goes a bit farther: to credit seals with supernatural qualities.

Over the years stories about seals have tended to merge with those which truly relate to the merfolk, some of which species are able to slough off their sealskins to assume a human form and, in their way, meet and mate with humans. Indeed, it is often difficult to distinguish between the two species, particularly as the semi-human aspect and the element of enchantment ride high as a characteristic feature in many tales.

There is the belief that drowned persons sometimes assume the form of sealmen and sealwomen, and are also able to lay aside their skins to become living humans again at night-time, though they must assume their former state by sunrise. The common elements in many tales include the seal woman laying aside her skin for some reason, often to groom or to bathe, and the skin being stolen and hidden by some fisherman. Captured thus for a time in human form, the erstwhile seal performs all the tasks and duties of a human wife, even to the extent of bearing children. Eventually the sealskin is discovered, usually the result of the unthinking act of a neighbour, the husband or one of the offspring; the skin is put on once more and the seal, in its former cast, is last seen slithering down to the shore and into the sea, while the humans left on land suffer their loss as best they can.

In 1894 the Revd Archibald MacDonald collected the poems and songs of John MacCodrum, the North Uist bard who died in 1796. He was regarded as being the last bard to the Lords of the Isles, an office to which he succeeded in 1763; he is buried at Hougharry, in North Uist. The Revd MacDonald wrote of a woman of the bard's lineage who "used to be seized with violent pains at the time of the annual seal hunt, out of sympathy, it was supposed, with her suffering relatives". The clan is now extinct, so far as is known, as there has been no person of that name living in Scotland for a considerable time. There are, however, MacOdrums living in Cape Breton Island.

The reason for the belief may lie in the seals' possession of several human characteristics such as their intelligent and expressive eyes, their ability to weep and, as some would have it, the ability to sing in a startlingly human fashion and the fact that, as Martin Martin was told, "they make their addresses to each other by kisses".

Apart from the MacCodrums, other families claimed descent from a seal woman, notably the MacCrimmons of Skye and the MacPhees of the island of Colonsay.

All burial places on North Uist are said to be so placed as to require the crossing of water to reach them. It cannot be said whether this is a relic of the times when islands in lochs were used as cemeteries in order to prevent wolves and other wild beasts from interfering with the corpses, or whether it is connected with the belief that evil spirits are unable to cross water, and thus the dead may be purged of all ill on their way to their last resting-place; in either case, the traditions seem to have been adhered to rigidly. The burial ground used by the people of the island of Boreray to the north of Machair Leathann was situated on the shore below Ard a Mhorain, looking towards the south tip of the island. A tradition has it that when one of the Boreray islanders died, and was subsequently interred with all due rites, seals were seen to come and congregate at the water's edge as if to pay their last respects to the deceased. No explanation was given for this phenomenon, except that it is well known that seals are a musical race and are fond of watching scenes of pomp and circumstance.

Seun This is more a term of the Highland occult than a being, though it is often applied to a person under its influence: an occult agency or supernatural power used to ward away injury and to protect invisibility. In this context it can be included here. It is supposed to be of Norse origin and one main story indicates its realm of influence.

The Norsemen, on one of their harrying expeditions, were beaten by the men from Gairloch, Wester Ross, who hotly pursued them as they retreated to their ships. Before the Norsemen leaped down from a rocky ledge and into their boats, the men threw down their arms in a heap, the leader touched the heap with his spear and, uttering some magic formula, caused the arms to disappear. The Norsemen then pulled out to sea, intending after dark to return for their arms and give the Gairloch men as good as they had received. But a storm blew up and the Norsemen were drowned. The place where the incident occurred is known as Uamh an Oir, the Cave of Gold. One person who saw it declared that at the innermost recess there appeared to be a beautiful stair. This hiding place opens only once in every seven years. It was also believed that if a fugitive struck the rock at this place with a hazel stick, it would open to receive him into safety; he would be released after darkness fell. Another condition was that the fugitive must not on any account look back, as a certain Neil MacLeod did when pursued by a MacKenzie. Poor Neil stood on the rock and looked around for his enemy, by whom he was at once shot. The usual cairn was raised above Neil and every MacKenzie must when passing spit on it if he wishes to be lucky. The cairn is a well-known landmark in the district and is known as the 'spittle cairn'.

The *Seun* was much in evidence during the Forty-five when French ships were trying to land arms and gold for the use of the Prince. On one occasion it was used to hide the kegs of gold landed on Isle Ewe. At that time a man named Macrae who was in possession of the *Seun* undertook to carry the kegs of the Prince, who was hiding in Skye. While travelling with them he was surprised by Royalists and, with his companions, ran down the deep gorge known as Fedan More. As the pursuers drew near he pronounced the magical words and the gold became invisible, but not the men, who were captured and put to death. The kegs are still there to this day. Once a year, however, at sunrise on 22 June they become visible. Some years ago a woman who was herding cows in this place saw the earth open and, as she knew what it meant, she stuck her staff at the spot and ran off for help. But when she returned with a few men, neither staff, opening nor kegs were to be seen. In later days the charm was possessed by a famous Gairloch smuggler called Alasdair the Hunter. At one time Alasdair was among the Minch fishermen measuring out whisky for sale, when there was a shout that a government customs boat was straight on their tracks. Alasdair, knowing that his own men had seen the cutter before the officials had seen them, got to work and uttered the magic formula to render his men and himself invisible. The cutter sailed right past them. When Alasdair ever wanted venison he stalked a deer, then became invisible and drove it to his croft, where he shot the beast—to save him the trouble of carrying it home.

Sluagh This supernatural phenomenon is the 'host of the air' and is related to fairy belief. The more mundane of the human species might attribute the *Sluagh* to a natural occurrence: the whirlwind that raises dust and straws on a perfectly still and calm evening. In Gaelic this disturbance is called *oiteag sluagh*. But to the more credulous, the disturbance is caused by the passage of a host of unseen beings. The *Sluagh*, in fact, is a throng of spirits of the dead which travels unseen through the air; it was something not to be encountered without some degree of fear.

One of the informants who communicated to Alexander Carmichael (of *Carmina Gadelica*) described this aerial throng: "They fly about in great clouds up and down the face of the earth, like starlings and come back to the scenes of their earthly transgressions. No soul of them is without clouds of earth, dimming the brightness of the works of God, nor can any win Heaven until a satisfaction is made for their sins on earth." A similar belief exists in Scandinavia; in Ireland the *Sliagh* are the fairies, for there fairy belief is closely interwoven with the spirits of the dead.

On bad nights the *Sluagh* are said to shelter themselves behind little docken stems and small yellow ragwort stalks. They often fight battles in the air and can be seen and heard on clear frosty nights advancing and retreating noisily one against the other. After a battle their crimson blood may be seen as stains on rocks and stones. *Fuil nan Sluagh*, the blood of the hosts, is the beautiful red 'crotal', of the rocks melted by frosts. The spirits are credited with the killing of cats, dogs, sheep and cattle with unerring darts. They also have the power to command humans to follow them, who have no alternative but to obey.

A man in Benbecula came under their influence. Night after night he would be carried to far-off places to be returned to his home the next morning completely exhausted. Eventually he would bar his door each night and on no account venture outside after dusk. When the whirling wind of the *Sluagh* blew past his house he experienced the greatest of mental struggles to keep himself from unbarring the door. A man in the island of Lismore used to suffer under the same conditions. More than once he would disappear from the midst of his companions and, as mysteriously, he would reappear the next morning, utterly exhausted and prostrate. He was under certain vows not to reveal what had occurred during these aerial travels.

The *Sluagh* are supposed to come from the west; therefore, when a person is dying, the door and windows on the west side of the house are secured to keep out the malicious spirits. Late last century a burial took place in Glen Creran, in Appin, at which, immediately the corpse had been lowered and earth closed over it, the funeral party smashed the bier against a tree in the burying ground, so that it would not be used in any attempt by the *Sluagh* to lure the dead away with it.

Of passing interest is the anglicised version of the cry of the spirit-host, *Sluagh-ghairm*, from which the word 'slogan' is derived.

Stic This is a fairy imp, somewhat akin to Puck, intent on all kinds of mischief done to hurt humans and for their irritation. Occasionally the name is given to a fairy demon. There were a number of variations of the species: evil imp, imp of the Devil, imp of the great demon, house imp and a doorstep imp. The latter two were the cause of mishaps in the house, like accidents, to which no rhyme or reason could be ascribed as to their occurrence. The doorstep imp was particularly adept at tripping up visitors as they entered the house—and who has not encountered them?

Tacharan This was a species of water-kelpie, distinctive because of its diminutive size, a dwarf among the water-beings.

Uraisg This being is not unlike the *Peallaidh* and frequents glens, corries, reedy lakes and streams. He is represented as a monster, half-man, half-goat, with abnormally long hair, long teeth and long claws. He is not, however, unfriendly to those who do not annoy him beyond showing them scenes and telling them of events above, upon and below the world that fill them with terror. Many places are called after the *Uraisg*. In the Cuillin Hills in Skye there is Coire nan Uraisg, and another adjoining it called Bealach nan Uraisg. Gleann Uraisg, a glen in Kilninver, in Argyll, carries the monster's name.

CHAPTER 8

The Power of Words

IN ALL RITUAL, CEREMONY, supplication and activity intended to invite the supernatural world to participate in securing some benefit for the future, the use of words is often of supreme importance. Through words the nature of the benefit can be improved; through the secrecy of words, the efficacy of a cure, for instance, can be transmitted through generations of healers; through the medium of words the mind can be convinced that unknown powers can be summoned for good or evil. The following is a necessarily brief selection of chants, rhymes, runes and charms used in the supernatural Highlands for a number of centuries. How old some of these examples are is not known, but they contain elements which at least echo an ancient past, and who can say they do not go back farther?

Birth and Baptism

A wavelet for thy form,
A wavelet for thy voice,
  A wavelet for thy sweet speech;

A wavelet for thy luck,
A wavelet for thy good,
  A wavelet for thy health;

A wavelet for thy throat,
A wavelet for thy pluck,
  A wavelet for thy graciousness;
  Nine waves for thy graciousness.

Prayer at Rising

Thou King of moon and sun,
  Thou King of stars beloved,
Thou knowest Thyself our need,
  O Thou merciful God of life.

Each day that we move,
  Each time that we awaken,
Causing vexation and gloom,
  To the King of Hosts who loved us.

Be with us through each day,
  Be with us through each night;
Be with us each night and day,
  Be with us each day and night.

Charm against Venom

Be the eye of God betwixt me and each eye,
The purpose of God betwixt me and each purpose,
The hand of God betwixt me and each hand,
The shield of God betwixt me and each shield,
The desire of God betwixt me and each desire,
The bridle of God betwixt me and each bridle,
  And no mouth can curse me.

Be the pain of Christ betwixt me and each pain,
The love of Christ betwixt me and each love,
The dearness of Christ betwixt me and each dearness,
The kindness of Christ betwixt me and each kindness,
The wish of Christ betwixt me and each wish,
The will of Christ betwixt me and each will,
  And no venom can wound me.

Be the might of Christ betwixt me and each might,
The right of Christ betwixt me and each right,
The flowing of Spirit betwixt me and each flowing,
The laving of Spirit betwixt me and each laving,
The bathing of Spirit betwixt me and each bathing,
  And no ill thing can touch me.

Prayer for Protection

O Father of Truth,
O Son of mercy,
Free us at this time,
Free us at every time.

Thou Son of God, grant me forgiveness
In my false swearing,
In my foolish deed,
In my empty talk.

Sain me from the hurt of the quiet women,
  Sain me from the hurt of the wanton women,
Sain me from the hurt of the fairy women,
  Sain me from the hurt of the world-women.

Prayer

I pray and supplicate
Cuibh and Columba,
  The Mother of my King,
Brigit womanly,
  Michael militant,
High-king of the angels,
  To succour and shield me
From each fay on earth.

Journey Prayer

God be with thee in every pass,
Jesus be with thee on every hill,
Spirit be with thee on every stream,
  Headland and ridge and lawn.

Each sea and land, each moor and meadow,
Each lying down, each rising up,
In the trough of the waves, on the crest of the billows,
  Each step of the journey thou goest.

The New Moon

Glory to thee for ever,
  Thou bright moon, this night;
Thyself art ever
  The glorious lamp of the poor.

The Sun

The eye of the great God,
The eye of the God of glory,
The eye of the King of hosts,
The eye of the King of the living,
  Pouring upon us
    At each time and season,
  Pouring upon us
    Gently and generously.

Glory to thee,
Thou glorious sun.

Glory to thee, thou sun,
Face of the God of life.

Smooring the Hearth

I will smoor the hearth
As Brigit the Fostermother would smoor.
The Fostermother's holy name
Be on the hearth, be on the herd,
Be on the household all.

Prayer for Seaweed

Produce of sea to land,
Produce of land to sea;
He who doeth not in time,
Scant shall be his share.

Seaweed being cast on shore
Bestow, Thou Being of bestowal;
Produce being brought to wealth,
O Christ, grant me my share.

The Club-moss

Thou man who travellest blithely,
Nor hurt nor harm shall befall thee
Nor in sunshine nor in darkness
If but the club-moss be on thy pathway.

The Pearlwort

I will cull the pearlwort
Beneath the fair sun of Sunday,
Beneath the hand of the Virgin,
In the name of the Trinity
Who willed it to grow.

While I shall keep the pearlwort,
Without ill mine eye,
Without harm my mouth,
Without grief my heart,
Without guile my death.

Repelling the Evil Eye

It is mine own eye
It is the eye of God,
It is the eye of God's Son
   Which shall repel this,
   Which shall combat this.

He who has made to thee the eye,
Surely lie it on himself,
Surely lie it on his affection,
Surely lie it on his stock.

On his wife, on his children,
On his means, on his dear ones,
On his cattle, on his seed,
And on his comely kine.

On the little fairy women
Who are reeling in the knoll,
Who are biding in the heath,
Who are filling the cavities.

Countering the Evil Eye

I am lifting a little drop of water
   In the holy name of the Father;
I am lifting a little drop of water
   In the holy name of the Son;
I am lifting a little drop of water
   In the holy name of the Spirit.

Shake from thee thy harm,
Shake from thee thy jealousy,
Shake from thee thine illness
   In the name of the Father,
   In the name of the Son,
   In the name of the Holy Spirit.

Charm of the Threads

I place the protection of God about thee,
Blind folk over thee;
Mayest thou be shielded from every peril;
May the Gospel of the God of grace
Be from thy crown to the ground about thee.
May men love thee
And women not work thee harm.

Eye charm for a Mote

The goading prick
Caught fast in rock,
Leap of belling elk,
The mote that is in the eye
Place, O King of life,
   Gently on my tongue.

Charm for Consumption

I trample on thee, evil wasting,
As tramples swan on brine,
Thou wasting of back, thou wasting of body,
Thou foul wasting of chest.

May Christ's own Gospel
Be to make thee whole,
The Gospel of the Healer of healers,
The Gospel of the God of Grace,

To remove from thee thy sickness
In the pool of health
From the crown of thy head
To the base of thy two heels,

From thy two loins thither
To thy two loins hither,
In reliance on the might of the God of love
And of the whole Powers together—
   The love of grace!

Charm for King's Evil

May God heal thee, my dear;
I am now placing my hand on thee
In the name of Father, in the name of Son, in the name of
   Spirit of Virtue,
Three Persons Who encompass thee ever.

Full healing be to thy red blood,
Perfect healing to thy soft flesh,
Another healing to thy white skin,
In the name of the powers of the Holy Three,
In the name of the powers of the Holy Three.

Charm of the Sprain

Bride went out
In the morning early,
With a pair of horses;
One broke his leg,
With much ado,
That was apart,
She put bone to bone,
She put flesh to flesh,
She put sinew to sinew,
She put vein to vein,
As she healed that
May I heal this.

Love Charm

It is not love knowledge to thee
To draw water through a reed,
But the love of him thou choosest,
With his warmth to draw to thee.

Arise thou early on the day of the Lord,
To the broad flat flag
Take with thee the biretta of a priest
And the pinnacled canopy.

Lift them on thy shoulder
In a wooden shovel,
Get thee nine stems of ferns
Cut with an axe,

The three bones of an old man,
That have been drawn from the grave,
Burn them on a fire of faggots,
And make them all into ashes.

Shake it into the very breast of thy lover,
Against the sting of the north wind,
And I will vow, and warrant thee,
That man will never leave thee.

The Catkin Wool

Pluck will I myself the catkin wool,
The lint the lovely Bride culled through her palm,

For success, for cattle, for increase,
For pairing, for uddering, for milking,
For female calves, white bellied,
As was spoken in the prophecy.

Omens

I heard the cuckoo with no food in my stomach,
I heard the stock-dove on the top of the tree,
I heard the sweet singer in the copse beyond,
And I heard the screech of the owl of the night.

  I saw the lamb with his back to me,
I saw the snail on the bare flag-stone,
I saw the foal with his rump to me,
I saw the wheatear on a dyke of holes,
I saw the snipe while sitting bent,
And I foresaw that the year would not
    Go well with me.

Sayings of Weekdays

That which is begun on Monday,
It will be quick or it will be slow.

Unlucky it is on early Monday
To go to the shearing of the maiden.

The expedition of Saturday to the north,
The expedition of Monday to the south,
Though I should only have the lamb,
It is on Monday I would go with it.

Never was Wednesday without sun,
Never was winter without gloom,
Never was New Year without flesh,
Never was wife willingly without son.

Friday for cutting,
Tuesday for growing.

Saturday without reproach, without borrowing, without debts,
End of a week gladsome, bright, sunshiny.

Enough is the new moon on Saturday,
Once in the seven years.

The child of the Lord's Day,
Even of step.

Go not on the Monday,
Move not on the Tuesday,
The Wednesday is false,
The Thursday dilatory,
Friday is unlucky, ·
Saturday is unloving,
Give up thy journey of misery;
Unseemly for thee to go tomorrow—
The Lord's Day is for peaceful rest.

Sunday is tribute to the King,
Monday arise not early,
Tuesday is war and death,
Wednesday is wounds and blood,
Thursday is hateful and evil,
Friday of dire ill-deed,
   Ill-timed to leave tonight.

Fairy Rune

God be between me and every fairy,
Every ill wish and every druidry,
Today is Thursday on sea and land,
I trust in the King that they do not hear me.

Charm Against witchcraft

A tuft of rowan twigs
From the face of Ailsa Craig,
Put a red thread and a knot on it,
And place it on the end of the sprinkler,
And though the witch of Endor came,
Allan could manage her.

Charms to Counteract Evil Eye

The eye that went over,
and came back,
That reached the bone,
And reached the marrow,
I will lift from off thee,
And the King of the Elements will aid me.

If eye has blighted,
Three have blessed,
Stronger are the Three that blessed,
Than the eye that blighted;
The Father, Son, and Holy Ghost;
If aught elfin or worldly has harmed it,
On earth above,
Or in hell beneath,
Do Thou, God of Grace, turn it aside.

Charm for General Use

Thou wilt be the friend of God,
And God will be thy friend;
Iron will be your two soles,
And twelve hands shall clasp thy head;
Thy afflictions be in tree or holly,
Or rock at sea,
Or earth on land;
A protecting shield be about thee,
Michael's shield be about thee;
Colum-Kil's close-fitting coat of mail
Protect thee from elfin bolts
And from the enclosures of pain,
From the trouble of this world
And the other world.
The woman, on her knee,
And on her eye,
On her choicest flesh,
And on the veins of her heart,
Till it reach the place whence it came.
Every jealous envious woman
That propagates her flesh and blood,
On herself be her desire, and envy, and malice.

The Fairy Lover

Why is not come the calf of my delight,
The calf of my delight, the calf of my delight;
Why is not come the calf of my delight,
    To keep the visit with me?

I was last night in the Meads of the Fold,
The Meads of the Fold, the Meads of the fold;
I was last night in the Meads of the Fold,
    Drinking beer with the beguiling one.

I'll be this night in the Meads of the Kine,
The Meads of the Kine, the Meads of the Kine;
I'll be this night in the Meads of the Kine,
   Eating the May-time crowdie.

Sad that I were not in the Meads of the Trees,
The Meads of the Trees, the Meads of the Trees;
Sad that I were not in the Meads of the Trees,
   With none there but my darling.

Sad that I were not in yonder glen,
In yonder glen, in yonder glen;
Sad that I were not in yonder glen,
   Where I fell in love with the beguiling one.

The Wind on New Year Eve

South wind—heat and produce,
North wind—cold and tempest,
West wind—fish and milk,
East wind—fruit on trees.

Reaping Blessing

God, bless Thou Thyself my reaping,
Each ridge and plain and field,
Each sickle curved, shapely, hard,
Each ear and handful in the sheaf
   Each ear and handful in the sheaf.

Bless each maiden and youth
Each woman and tender youngling
Safeguard them beneath Thy shield of strength,
And gird them in the house of the saints,
   Gird them in the house of the saints.

Encompass each goat, sheep and lamb,
Each cow and horse and store
Surround Thou the flocks and herds,
And tend them to a kindly fold,
   And tend them to a kindly fold.

For the sake of Michael, head of hosts,
Of Mary, fair-skinned branch of grace,
Of Bride, smooth-white of ringletted locks,
Of Columba of the graves and tombs,
Of Columba of the graves and tombs.

Bibliography

AS WILL BE APPRECIATED, much of the traditions and folklore of the Highlands is locked away in the Gaelic language and is therefore inaccessible in its original form to those who have no knowledge of the tongue. However, there is a great deal available in English to those who have both the interest and the will to seek out the varied patterns of the folk-weave of the region. The bibliography has been made intentionally comprehensive so that readers may follow whichever facet of the supernatural Highlands appeals to them. It will be noticed that many interesting articles appear in the journals of such institutions of the Folklore Society and the Gaelic Society of Inverness; their proceedings are usually available in most libraries, but if not, can be obtained through the library request services. The extent of the bibliography will indicate the wide range and vast ground covered by folklore and tradition, suggesting, as is in fact the case, that the Highland region of Scotland, while at present a part of a much larger national whole, is a distinct area with a distinctive culture which still offers the enthusiast and sympathetic researcher much new ground to discover and to enjoy.

ANON *The History of Witches, Ghosts and Highland Seers* (Berwick, 1803)
ANWYL, E. *Celtic Religion in Pre-Christian Times* (London, 1906)

BAIN, C. *The Lordship of Petty* (Nairn, 1925)
BANKS, M. M. *British Calendar Customs* (3 vols) (The Folklore Society, London, 1937–41)
BEITH, M. *Healing Threads* (Edinburgh, 1995)
'B.J.' *Highland Pearls* (Gairloch, Ross-shire, 1972)
BLACK, C. *A Calendar of Cases of Witchcraft, 1510–1727, in Scotland* (New York, 1938)
BOSWELL, J. *A Journal of a Tour to the Hebrides with Samuel Johnson, L.L.D.,* (ed. T. Ratcliffe Barnet) (London, 1928)
BRUCE-WATT, J. *Selected Highland Folk Tales* (Edinburgh, 1961)
— *More Highland Folk Tales* (Edinburgh, 1964)
BRUFORD, A. 'Scottish Gaelic Witch Stories—a provisional type list' (Scottish Studies, vol. 11, pt 1, 1967)
BULLOCH, J. *The Life of the Celtic Church* (Edinburgh, 1963)

CALDER, C. C. (ed.) *Folk Tales and Fairy Lore* (Edinburgh, 1910)
CAMERON. E. *A Highland Chapbook* (Stirling, 1928)
CAMERON, F. R. *Told in Furthest Hebrides* (Stirling, 1936)
CAMPBELL, A. *Waifs and Strays of Celtic Tradition* (London, 1891)
CAMPBELL, E. M. *The Search for Morag, 1972* (London, 1972)
CAMPBELL, J. F. *Popular Tales of the West Highlands* (Edinburgh, 1860–62)
CAMPBELL, J. G. *Superstitions of the Scottish Highlands* (Glasgow, 1900)
— *Witchcraft and Second Sight in the Scottish Highlands* (Glasgow, 1902)
CAMPBELL, J. L. *Tales of Barra, Told by the Coddy* (Edinburgh, 1961)
— (ed.) *A Collection of Highland Rites and Customs* (London, 1975)
— & THOMSON, D. *Edward Llhuyd in the Scottish Highlands, 1699–1700* (Oxford, 1963)
—& HALL, T. H. *Strange Things* (London, 1968)
CAMPBELL, M. *The Dark Twin* (novel) (London & Inverness, 1973)
CARMICHAEL, A. *Carmina Cadelica* (6 vols) (Edinburgh, 1900–70)
   Celtic Magazine, 13 volumes (Inverness, 1875–88)
   Celtic Monthly, 25 volumes (Glasgow, 1893–1917)
   Celtic Review, 10 volumes (Edinburgh, 1904–16)
CHADWICK, N. *The Druids* (Cardiff, 1966)
CHRISTIANSEN, R. T. 'Gaelic and Norse Folklore' (*Folk-liv*, 2)
COHN, N. *Europe's Inner Demons* (London, 1975)
CROW, W. B. *The Occult Properties of Herbs* (London, 1969)

DALYELL, J. G. *The Darker Superstitions of Scotland* (Edinburgh, 1834)
DAVIDSON, T. *Rowan Tree and Red Thread* (Edinburgh, 1949)
DINSDALE ,T. *Loch Ness Monster* (London, 1961)
DOUGAL, J. W. *Island Memories* (Edinburgh, 1937)
DOUGLAS, Sir G. *Scottish Fairy and Folk Tales* (London, 1918)
DREVER, H. *The Lure of the Kelpie* (Edinburgh, 1937)
DUKE, J. A. *The Columban Church* (Edinburgh, 1957)

Folklore, Journal of the Folklore Society:
   Vol. 1 (1883) 'Superstition in Stornoway'
                   'Ancient Superstitions in Tiree'
         2 (1886) 'Witchcraft in Skye'(J. Frazer)
         6 (1888) 'The Folklore of Sutherlandshire' (Miss Dempster)
                   'Some Folklore from Achternead (Ross)' (W. Gregor)
         7 (1889) 'Sutherlandshire Folklore' (J. Frazer)

         New Series:
   Vol. 1 (1890) 'A Highland Folktale and its Origin in Custom'
                      (G. Gomme)
                   'Highland Superstitions in Inverness-shire' (J. Frazer)
         3 (1892) 'The Baker of Beauly' (Highland Version of the Three Precepts) (W. Clouston)
         4 (1893) 'The Sanctuary of Mourie (Ross)' (G. Godden)
         6 (1895) 'Notes on Beltane Cakes (from various places in the Highlands)' (W. Gregor)

'Harvest Custom in Bernera, Lewis' (R. C. MacLagan)
'Traditions, Customs and Superstitions of Lewis'
(J. Abercromby)
'Notes on Folklore Objects collected in Argylleshire'
(R. C. MacLagan)

7 (1896) 'Folklore from the Hebrides' (M. MacPhail)
8 (1897) 'Ghost Lights of the West Highlands' (R. C. MacLagan)
'Folklore from the Hebrides' (M. MacPhail)
9 (1898) 'Some Highland Folklore' (W. Craigie)
'Folklore from the Hebrides' (M. MacPhail)
10 (1899) 'The Powers of Evil in the Outer Hebrides'
(A. Goodrich Freer)
11 (1900) 'Folklore from the Hebrides' (M. MacPhail)
13 (1902) 'More Folklore from the Hebrides' (A. Goodrich Freer)
14 (1903) 'Highland Fisherfolk and their Superstitions'
(M. Cameron)
'Charms, etc. from the Highlands' (R. C. MacLagan)
'Folklore from the Hebrides' (A. Goodrich Freer)
'Old-world Survivals in Ross-shire' (S. MacDonald)
21 (1910) 'Scraps of Scottish Folklore' (S. MacDonald)
25 (1914) 'The Keener (banshee) in the Scottish Highlands and
Islands' (R. C. MacLagan)
32 (1921) 'The Mingling of Fairy and Witch Beliefs in 16th and
17th Century Scotland' (J. McCulloch)
33 (1922) 'Folklore from the Isle of Skye'(J. McCulloch)
34 (1923) 'Folklore from the Isle of Skye'(J. McCulloch)
36 (1925) 'Gaelic Folktale' (J. G. MacKay)
39 (1928) 'Scottish Examples of Confusion in Custom, Beliefs and
Names' (M. M. Banks)
42 (1931) 'A Hebridean version of Colum Cille and St Oran'
(M. M. Banks)
43 (1932) 'Scots Folklore Scraps' (H. Rose)
45 (1934) 'Folk-lore Notes from Scotland' (M. M. Banks)
49 (1938) 'The Last Sheaf in the Island of Vallay, of N. Uist' (N. M.)
'Stray Notes on Scottish Folklore' (D. Rorie)
50 (1939) 'A Tale from Mid-Curr (Strathspey)' (V. Ross)
52 (1941) 'Fires Put Out (By Bailiff) before Eviction (in Lewis)'
(V. Ross)
62 (1951) 'Scraps of Highland Folklore' (E. Begg)
63 (1952) 'Scraps of Highland Folklore' (E. Begg)
68 (1957) 'Folklore and Tradition in N. Uist'(B. Megaw)
72 (1961) 'Some Late Accounts of the Fairies' (K. M. Briggs)
75 (1964) 'A Prospect of Fairyland' (S. Sanderson)
76 (1965) 'Notes on Lore and Customs in the Districts near
Portnahaven, Rhinns of Islay' (F. Celoria)
84 (1973) 'The Science of Fairy Tales' (A. Jackson)

FRAZER, J. *Deuteroscopia; or a Brief Discourse concerning the Second Sight* (Edinburgh, 1707) reprinted in 1820 in *A Collection of Rare and Curious Tracts on Witchcraft and the Second Sight*
FRAZER, J. G. *The Golden Bough* (London, 1913)

Gaelic Society of Inverness, *Transactions*:
Vol. 3/4 'The Prophecies of the Brahan Seer' (A. MacKenzie)
6 'The Collecting of Highland Legends' (W. Watson)
7 'Gaelic Names of Trees, Shrubs and Plants' (C. Ferguson)
9 'The Strathglass Witches' (W. MacKay)
10 'Celtic Mythology' (A. MacBain)
14 'Highland Ghosts' (A. MacDonald)
'Highland Superstitions' (A. MacBain)
'Popular Medicine in the Highlands' (D. Masson)
14/15 'The Sheiling—Its Traditions and Songs' (M. MacKellar)
17 'Gaelic Incantations' (W. MacBain)
18 'Apparitions and Ghosts of the Isle of Skye' (N. Matheson)
'Gaelic Incantations and Charms in the Hebrides'
(W. MacKenzie)
'Some Highland Fishermen's Fancies' (A. Polson)
19 'Religion and Mythology of the Celts' (A. MacDonald)
'Stray Customs and Legends' (J. MacDonald)
21 'Fauns and Fairies'(J. MacDonald)
'Second Sight in the Highlands' (A. Goodrich Freer)
22 'The Luck of Highland Folklore' (A. Polson)
25/27 'Breadalbane Folklore' (J. MacDonald)
26 'Ancient Celtic Deities' (E. Anwyl)
29 'Mythological Beings in Gaelic Folklore' (C. Diechkoff)
'Second Sight' (D. MacEchern)
31 'The Life and Literary Labours of the Rev. Robert Kirk
of Aberfoyle'
32 'Gaelic Names of Plants: Studies of their Uses and Lore'
(A. MacFarlane)
32/33 'Social Customs of the Gael' (A. MacDonald)
'Gaelic Seasons' (A. MacDonald)
34 'Myths associated with Mountains, Springs and Lochs in the
Highlands' (A. MacFarlane)
39/40 'Medicine Among the Gaelic Celts' (J. J. Galbraith)
42 'Death Divination in Scottish Folk Tradition' (C. I. MacLean)
44 'The Folklore Elements in "Carmine Gadelica"
(F. G. Thompson)
46 'The Historical Coinneach Odhar' (W. Matheson)

GILLIES, H. C. *Regimen Sanitatis. The Rule of Health* (A Gaelic MS of the Early 16th Century) (Glasgow, 1911)
GORDON-CUMMING, C. F. *In the Hebrides* (London, 1886)

GRANT, I. F. *Everyday Life on an Old Highland Farm, 1769–82* (London, 1924)
— *Highland Folkways* (London, 1961)
GRANT, K. *Myth, Tradition and Story from Western Argyll* (N. D.)
GUNN, NEIL M. *Second Sight* (a novel) (London, 1940)

HADINGHAM, E. *Ancient Carvings in Britain: A Mystery* (London, 1974)
HARRISON, C. B. (ed.) *Newes from Scotland* (1591) (New York, 1966)
HARRISON, M. *The Roots of Witchcraft* (London, 1972)
HENDERSON, C. *Survivals in Belief among the Celts* (Glasgow, 1911) *Highland Monthly*, 5 volumes (Inverness, 1889–93)
HOLIDAY, F. W. *The Great Orm of Loch Ness* (London, 1968)
— The Dragon and the Disc (London, 1973)

INSULANUS, THEOPHILUS (Revd Macpherson, Skye?) *A Treatise on the Second Sight* (Edinburgh, 1703) also in *Miscellenea Scotia*, III
Inverness Courier, 'The Assynt Murder' (report involving dreams) (Inverness, October 1831)
Inverness Field Club, *Transactions*: 'Sea Myths and Lore of the Hebrides' (A. MacFarlane) (volume 9)

JAMES VI *Daemonologie* (London, 1603)

KIRK, R. *The Secret Commonwealth of Elves, Fauns and Fairies* (MS dated 1691) (Edinburgh, 1815; edition edited by R. B. Cunningham-Grahame, Stirling, 1933)

LANG, A. *The Book of Dreams and Ghosts* (London, 1900)
LINTON, E. L. *Witch Stories* (London, 1861 and 1972)

MACBAIN, A. *Celtic Mythology and Religion* (Stirling, 1917)
MACCULLOCH, J. A. *Eddic Mythology: The Religion of the Ancient Celts* (Edinburgh, 1911)
MACDONALD, A. *Story and Song From Lochness-side* (Inverness, 1914)
MACDONALD, D. *Tales and Traditions of the Lews* (Stornoway, 1967)
MACDONALD, J. N. *Shinty* (Inverness, 1932)
MACDONALD, K. N. *The MacDonald Bards* (Inverness, 1911)
MACDONALD, M. 'Two Brahan Seers' (*Scots Magazine*, October 1969)
MACDOUGALL, J. *Folk Tales and Fairy Lore* (Edinburgh, 1910)
— *Folk Hero Tales* (London, 1891)
MACGREGOR, A. *Highland Superstitions* (Stirling, 1951)
MACGREGOR, A. A. *The Peatfire Flame* (Edinburgh, 1937)
— *The Ghost Book* (London, 1955)
— *Phantom Footsteps* (London, 1959)
MACKAY, J. G. *More West Highland Tales* (Edinburgh, 1951)
MACKAY, W. *Urquhart and Glenmoriston* (Inverness, 1913)

MACKENDRICK, T. N. *The Druids* (London, 1974)

MACKENZIE, A. *A Gallery of Ghosts* (London, 1972)

MACKENZIE, A. *The Prophecies of the Brahan Seer* (Inverness, 1896; reprinted, Golspie, 1972)

MACKENZIE, D. A. *Scottish Myth and Legend* (London, N.D.)

MACKENZIE, O. *A Hundred Years in the Highlands* (London, 1921; reprinted, London, 1974)

MACLAGAN, R. C. *Evil Eye in the Western Islands* (London, 1902)

— *The Games and Diversions of Argyllshire* (London, 1891)

MACLEAN, A. SINCLAIR *The Glenbard Collection of Gaelic Poetry*

MACLEAN, C. I. *The Highlands* (London, 1959; reprinted, Inverness, 1975)

— 'Traditional Beliefs in Scotland' (Scottish Studies, vol. 3, pt 2, 1959)

MACLEAN, G. R. D. *Poems of the Western Highlanders* (London, 1961)

MACLELLAN, A. (ed. J. L. Campbell) *Stories from South Uist* (London, 1961)

MACLENNAN, A. B. *The Petty Seer* (2nd edition, Inverness, 1906)

MACLEOD, D. J. *Highland Folklore* (Inverness, 1930)

MACNEILL, F. M. *The Silver Bough*, 3 vols (Glasgow, 1957–61)

MACNEILL, M. *The Festival of Lughnasa* (London, 1962)

MACRAE, N. *Highland Second Sight* (Dingwall, 1908)

MACRITCHIE, D. *The Testimony of Tradition* (London, 1893)

— *Fians, Fairies and Picts* (London, 1893)

MAIR, L. *Witchcraft* (London, 1969)

MARTIN, M. *A Description of the Western Isles of Scotland* (Edinburgh, 1703; Stirling, 1934)

MILLER, H. *Scenes and Legends from the North of Scotland* (Edinburgh, 1874)

MONTER, E. W. (ed.) *European Witchcraft* (London & New York, 1966)

MORRISON, N. *Superstitions of Lewis* (Stornoway, c. 1930)

— *Hebridean Lore and Romance* (Glasgow, 1936)

MURRAY, A. *Father Allan's Island* (London, 1936)

MURRAY, M. *The Witch-cult in Western Europe* (Oxford, 1962)

NAPIER, J. *Folklore or Superstitious Beliefs in the West of Scotland*

NICOLSON, A. *Gaelic Proverbs* (Edinburgh, 1884; Glasgow, 1951)

PIGGOTT, S. *The Druids* (London, 1968)

PITCAIRN, R. *Criminal Trials* ... (Edinburgh, 1933)

POLSON, A. *Highland Folklore Heritage* (Inverness, 1926)

— *Scottish Witchcraft Lore* (Inverness, 1932)

POWELL, T. G. E. *The Celts* (London 8r New York, 1958)

RHYS, SIR J. *Celtic Folklore* (Oxford, 1901)

ROBERTSON, R. M. *Selected Highland Folktales* (Edinburgh, 1961)

ROSS, J. 'The Sub-literary Tradition in Scottish Gaelic Song-poetry' (*Eigse*, vol. VII, 1953–55, Dublin)

SCOT, R. *The Discoverie of Witchcraft*, 1584 (London, 1964)

SCOTT, SIR W. *Letters on Demonologie and Witchcraft*, 1830 (London, 1884)

SETH, R. *In the Name of the Devil* (London, 1969)

SHARPE, K. *Witchcraft in Scotland* (London, 1884; reprinted 1972)

SHAW, M. F. *Folksongs and Folklore of South Uist* (London, 1955)

SIMPSON, W. D. *The Celtic Church in Scotland* (Edinburgh, 1935)

SJOESTEDT, M. L. *Dieux et Heros des Celtes* (Paris, 1940) (translated M. Dillon, London, 1949)

SPENCE, L. *The Magic Arts in Celtic Britain* (London, 1945)

STEWART, W. G. *Popular Superstitions and Festive Amusements of the Highlanders of Scotland* (Edinburgh, 1823)

'STREAMLINE' *Foretold* (Stirling, 1934)

SUMMERS, M. *The History of Witchcraft and Demonology* (London and New York, 1926)

Survey Committee, Report of Loch Morar Survey (London, 1970)

SUTHERLAND, E. *The Seer of Kintail* (a novel) (London, 1974)

SWIRE, O. *The Highlands and their Legends* (Edinburgh, 1963)

— *The Inner Hebrides and their Legends* (London, 1964)

— *The Outer Hebrides and their Legends* (Edinburgh, 1966)

THOMPSON, F. *The Ghosts, Spirits and Spectres of Scotland* (Aberdeen, 1973)

UNDERWOOD, C. *The Pattern of the Past* (London, 1973)

UNDERWOOD, P. A. *Gazetteer of British Ghosts* (London, 1971)

WATSON, L. *Supernature* (London, 1973)

WELBY, D. *Signs Before Death* (London, 1825)

WENTZ, W. Y. E. *The Fairy Faith in Celtic Countries* (Oxford, 1911)

Index

Aberdeen Witches, trial 21
Aberfeldy 128
Ach-na-Creige 123
Acts, repealed 29
Agriculture, Dept of 42
Am Fiosaiche Ileach
    see Islay Seer
Amish Moor 72
appetisers 79–80
Appin, Glen Creran 132–3
Applecross 90
apples 76
Ardersier 59
Ardincaple 104
Argyll 34
Arran,
    Bennan (West) 125
    Easter Sunday 91
ash 81
Ash Wednesday 90
atomic energy plant 63
Aubrey, John 48, 53–4
August 97
Auldearn 25–6

Badenoch,
    Clunie 54
    Laggan 30–1
    witchcraft 32
Bainisg 102
Ballachulish 73
Balnagowan, Lady 22–4
Banshee 18
baptism 134

Barra,
    Dealan-de 108
    fairy rhyme 113
    Glaistig 123
Bas Sona 86
Bealach a'Sgail 118
Bean-nighe 102–3
Beastie Loch 111
Beatons 78–9
Beinn Bhreac 118
Beithir 103
Beltane 10, 94–5
Benbecula,
    Cu sith 108
    Loireag 126
    merfolk 127–8
    Sluagh 132
Benmore 91, 126
Bennan (West) 125
Bernera,
    fairies 119
    harvest 93
Berneray, brownie of 105
birth 85, 134
Black Isle 62
black witchcraft 20–1
blaeberry 79
Blest, Isles of 68–9
blood-staunching 82
Blue Men of the Minch 103–4
Bochdan 104
bog-bean 80
Boniface VIII, Pope 15
Boreray 130
Borgie 32–3

Boswell, James 56–7
Brahan Castle 65
Brahan Seer 24, 45, 49, 60–6
Breadalbane 78
Breadhead, Janet 25–6
Briggs, Katherine 120
Broadford 73–4
brochan 90
brownies 104–5, 124
Buchan, John 9
buidseach 18

Caesar 11, 68
Cailleach 92–3, 94
Cailleach-uisge 105
Cairbre 105–6
Cairm 78
cal dheanntag 77
cal duilisg 77
Calluinn 99–100
Campbell, Revd 103
Campbeltown 38–9, 40
cancer-wort 79
Caoilte 69
Caoineag 106
Cape Breton Island 130
Cape Wrath 70
Carinish 43
Carmichael, Alexander
   see Carmina Gadelica
Carmina Gadelica 83–5, 88,
   113, 132
casg fola 82
Castle Lachlan 104
catkin wool 140–1
Ceasg 106
cereals 75
Chambers, R 27
changeling 107
Chanonry 24, 61, 65
chants 134–44
charms 134–44
   see also snaithe
Chisolm of Comar 27

Christmas 99
cinquefoil 77
Clach Toll 62
Clanranald of the Isles 62
clay images 32
club-moss 79, 137
Clunie 54
cock-fighting 90
Coinneach Odhar see Brahan
   Seer
Colonsay 104, 130
comfrey 79
Conall 107
consumption 139
corp creadh 32
counter-irritants 79
Creibh Mhor 22–3
Crodh-mara 107
Cu sith 107–8
Cuchillin's ghost 69
Culloden, Battle of 48, 62
Cupid 107
Cur nan Corran 93
cures,
   evil eye 41–4
   medical 78–82

da-shealladh
   see second sight
Dalyell, Christian Neil 24
dandelion 80
Däniken, Erich van 13
Day of the Big Porridge 90
Day of Little Christmas 100
Day of St Columba 98
Day of the three suppers 97
Dealan-de 108
death 85–6
deities 105–6, 122
déjà vu 46
delf-heal 80
Deuchair Chorran 93–4
Diana 14
Diodorus 68

divination 93
dog-violet 79
Dona 31
Dounreay 63
Dressing, Prayer at 83–4
Druids 10–11, 76–7
Duffus, King 20–1
duilseag 77
dulse broth 77
Dumbarton Rock 21
dwarf cornel 79–80

Each uisge 108–12
Earrach 96
Easdale 104
Easter Sunday 91
Edinburgh University 72
Eigg 49
emetics 79
Ensay 52, 106
Eolas 19, 37
Ercildoune, Thomas of 21
Eriskay 74
Erista 116
evictions 63
evil eye 35–44, 138, 142–3

Fairburn, MacKenzies of 64
fairies 112–21
    Queen of Fairy 21
    rhymes 142, 143–4
fairy dogs 107
fairy imps 133
fairy mouse 126
Farr 71
Fath-fith 121
Fearn 128
Fearn Abbey 103
febrifuges 79
February 97
Fergus, ghost of 69
fig-wort 79
Fionn 121
fir club-moss 79

Fogharach 96
folklore 75–87
    definition 12
Forbes, Lord President 48
Forres 21
Fortrose 24, 61
Forty-five 131
Foulis, Lady 23–4
foxgloves 81
Fraser, Annie 44
Fraticelli 14
Frazer, Revd John 49–51
Free Church 57
Frid 121–2
Friday 98
fruit and nuts 76
Fuath 121
funerals 73

Gainisg 122
Gairloch,
    Loch a Druing 120–1
    Seun 130–1
Galson 70
garden-sage 80
Geamradh 96
Geller, Uri 37
Ghillie Dhu 120–1
ghosts 67–74
Gigha 104
Glaistig 122–4
Glamis, Lady 21–2
Glen Creran 132–3
Glen Langavat 110
Glen Liadail 122
Glenborrodale 123
Glencoe, Massacre of 106
gluttony-plant 79
gnomes 121–2
Gobhar bacach 124
golden-rod 79
Good Friday 91
Gowdie, Isobel 21, 25–6
grave-cloths 47

Grimsay 41
groundsel 79
Gruagach 124-6

Halistra 51-2
Halloween 76, 96
Hallowmass 95-6
Harris,
    Easter Sunday 91
    Ensay 52, 106
    second sight 48
harvest 92-4, 96
    see also reaping
hazlenuts 76
heal-all 80
hearth, smooring 137
Hebrides,
    evil eye 38
    fairies 120
    St Patrick's Day 97
Heisgeir 124
hemlock 80
henbane 80
herbs 75, 76
Heynish 38
Hogmanay 99
Holiday, F.W. 103, 112
Horne, Janet 28-9
Hougharry 102, 130
house-leek 79

Imbolc 10
imps 133
Invergarry Castle 104
Inverness,
    blood staunching 82
    prediction 63
    witchcraft 22
Inverness-shire,
    Kiltarlity 44
    witchcraft 32
Invocation for Justice 87
Iona,
    mermaids 128

Palm Sunday 90
irritants, counter 79
Islay,
    fairies 120
    seer 61-2
Isle Ewe 131

James IV, King 21
Johnson, Samuel 48, 56-7, 92
journeys, prayer 136
justice, Invocation for 87

kelpies 18, 103-4, 108-9
    water 133
Kennedy, Dr John 57
kidney-vetch 79
Kilmuir 124-5
Kiltarlity 44
King's Evil 79
    charm 139
Kintail 116-17
Kintyre 50
Kirk, Robert 48, 113, 114, 120
Kirkhill 26-7
Knights Templar 15
knowledge 19, 37

Laggan, Good Wife of 30-1
Lame Goat 92-3, 124
Lammas 92
Latha a'Bhais 85-6
Laxdale 66
Lent 89-90
Lethbridge, J.C. 13
Lewis,
    Bernera 93, 119
    Galson 70
    Loch Erisort 73
    Loch Roag 33, 110, 115,
        117-18
    Mangersta 117
    Ness 70
    Palm Sunday 90
    Uig 116

Lianachan 124
Lightfoot 78, 81
Lismore 132
Loch Awe 39
Loch Carron 92
Loch a Druing 120–1
Loch Duvat 111
Loch Erisort 73
Loch Langavat 110
Loch Morar 112
Loch na Mna 111–12
Loch Ness 111, 112
Loch Roag 33, 110, 115,
    117–18
Loch Slin 102–3
Lochaber, Lianachan 124
Lochan nan Dubh Breac 126–7
Lochboisdale (South) 74
Loireag 126
Loncart, Lasky 23–4
Loth 28–9
lovage 79
love, charm 140
Luch-sith 126
Lugnasad 10
Luideag 126–7

Macaskill, Christina 52–3
MacBeths 78
MacCodrum, Clan 129, 130
MacCrimmons 130
MacDonald, Fr Allan 49, 74,
    111
MacDonald, Revd Archibald
    130
MacGillimondan, William 24
Macgregor, Alasdair Alpin
    73–4
Macillmertin, Sandy 22
MacIngarach, Marion 24
MacKay, Revd Thomas 71
Mackenzie, Kenneth see Brahan
    Seer
Mackenzie, Neil 131

MacKenzie, Osgood 120
MacKenzies of Fairburn 64
MacKinnon, Donald 51
MacLagan, Dr R.C. 37–8
MacLaren, Clan 128
MacLean, Calum I. 42, 128
Macleans 26–7
MacLeod, Sir Norman 105
MacMillan, John 24
MacOdrums 130
MacPhees 130
Mangersta 117
Mar, Earl and Lady of 21
March 97
Marshall, Edward 37
Martin, Martin 48, 49, 78, 79,
    106, 107, 130
Matheson, Man of the Ring
    32–3
May 91
meadow-rue 79
medicine see cures
medicos 82
Melon Udrigil 111
merfolk and mermaids 127–8,
    129
Michaelmas 76
Mikhailova, Nelya 37, 42
milfoil 81
Millburn 22–3
Miller, Donald Moir
    MacPherson 22
Miller, Hugh 127
Minch, Blue Men of the 103–4
Mingulay 113
mistletoe 77
Monday 98
moon 76
prayer 136
Morrison, Revd John 58–60
Morvern, North 123
motes, eye charm 139
Moydart 83
Muck 128

Mull,
Ach-na-Creige 123
Loch na Mna 111–12
Sound of 50, 123
Mungan 69
Munro, Hector 23–4
Munro, Robert 23–4
Munro, William 127
Murray, Dr Margaret 14

naiads 106
Nairn 25, 26
Nature 75, 83, 84
Ness 70
nettle broth 77
New Year's Day 99–100
New Year's Eve 99, 144
Newton Ferry 66
night-weed 80
Nin-Gilbert, Margaret 27–8
Nollaig 99
North Sea oil 63
Norway, King of 31
Nunton 62
nymphs 102–3

oats 75
Oban Times,
second sight 48
witchcraft 29–30
occult 121, 130
oil, North Sea 63
Old Culpeper 79
Oldshoremore 70
Olsen, Margaret 28
omens 141
Orkney 129
Ossian 121

Pabbay 115
Palm Sunday 90
Paterson, witch-finder 26–7
Peallaidh 128
pearlwort 137

Pennant, Thomas 48
Pepys, John 55–6
Pepys, Samuel 48
Perthshire 95
Petty 59
petty spurge 80
Pickering, Thomas 20
plants 76–80
Pluscardine, Barony of 65
porridge 90
Powell, T.G.E. 10
prayers 134–44
dressing 83–4
predictions *see* second sight
Prestonpans, Battle of 48
produce 38
prophecies *see* second sight
protection, prayer for 135–6
proverbs 35, 80
psychokinesis 36

Raasay 92
reaping, blessing 144
Reay, Lord 55–6
rhymes 134–44
ring dance 94
rising, prayers at 84, 134–5
Ross, Christina 23–4, 24
Ross, Katherine *see* Lady Foulis
Ross-shire,
Breadalbane 78
Fearn 128
Tarbet 40
witchcraft 27
rowan 81
Roy, Agnes 24
runes 134–44

sailors 33
St Bride's Day 97
St Bridget 87
St Brigit, Feast of 10
St Columba 80, 86
Day of 98

St Finan's Eve 97
St John's wort 80
St Kilda 66
St Patrick 21, 69
St Patrick's Day 97
St Peter 86
Samhainn 10, 76, 95–6
Samhradh 96
Sandwood Bay 70
Saturday 99
Saussure, Necker de 48
School of Scottish Studies 11,
     13, 42
Scott, Sir Michael 21
Scott, Sir Walter 14, 48
Scottish Calendar Customs 89
scurvy grass 79
sea-cows 107
Seaforth, House of 61, 64–5
seals 129–30
seaplant 78
seaweed, prayer for 137
second sight 45–66
seers *see* Brahan Seer; Islay Seer
serpents 103
Seun 130–1
Sharpe, Kirkpatrick 48
Shetland 129
Shrove Tuesday 89–90
Sian 19
Silver Bough 89
silverweed 77
     Year of the Silverweed Roots
     98
Sithean 119
Skye,
     Broadford 73, 73–4
     Conall 107
     fairies 119–20
     Glenborrodale 123
     Kilmuir 124–5
     last sheaf 93
     Loch Duvat 111

Lochan nan Dubh Breac
     126–7
Sleat 69
Sluagh 132–3
Smith, Mona 120
snaithe 42
Society for Physical Research
     48–9, 72
Soisgeul 19–20
songs, work 86–7
sorrel 77
Sound of Mull 50, 123
spearwort 79
spells, medical 81
sprains, charm 140
spring 96
sprites 122–3
     water 126
Stic 133
Stornoway,
     ghosts 71–2
     witchcraft 33
Strathnaver 32, 55
Strathpeffer 64
Strom Dearg 74
summer 96
sun, prayer 136–7
Sunday 98
superstition 18, 19, 35, 37
     definition 12–13
     evil eye 37
Sutherland,
     Each uisge 109
     Farr 71
     Lairg 71
     shortest day 97
     Strathnaver 55
Swire, Otta 125–6

tachar 46
Tacharan 133
taghairm 47
taibhs 46
Tain 29

tamhasg 46
tannas 46
taradh 46
taran 47
Tarbat, Lord 56
Tarbet 40
tasg 47
taslaich 46
Teagasg *see* Eolas
Teine Eigin 94
telekinesis 36
Thomas the Rhymer 62
threads, charm 138
Thursday 98
Tir nan Og 68–9
Tiree,
    Colonsay 104, 130
    Fridays 98–9
    Heynish 38
    second sight 49–51
    Year of the Silverweed Roots
        98
Tobermory 50
tonics 79–80
toradh 38
Torridon 33–4
trefoil 80
trials, witch 20–1
Tuesday 98
Tulloch, laird of 62

Uig 110, 116
Uist (North),
    Bealach a'Sgail 118
    evil eye 41, 42
    Heisgeir 124
    Hougharry 102, 130
    Peallaidh 129
    prediction 66
Uist (South),
    evil eye 40

ghosts 74
Glen Liadail 122
Uists, Easter Sunday 91
Uraisg 133
Urquharts of Cromarty 62

venom, charm against 135
vetch 77
    kidney 79
vulneraries 79

Waldensians 14
Wardlaw 26
washing 102
Waternish, Halistra 51–2
Wednesday 98
weekdays 98, 141–2
Wester Ross,
    Applecross 90
    blood staunching 82
    Gairloch 120–1, 130–1
    Melon Udrigill 111
    Torridon 33
Whistling Week 97
Whit Sunday 91–2
white helleborine 79
white witchcraft 18, 19–20, 44
winter 96
witch hunts 15–16
witchcraft 14–34
    charm against 142
wood sanicle 79
wood violet 79
work songs 86–7
wraiths 47

yarrow 79, 81, 82
Year of the Big Sheep 98
Year of the Silverweed Roots
    98
Yule 99

Crofting Years

FRANCIS THOMPSON

'I would recommend this book to all who are interested in the past, but even more so to those who are interested in the future survival of our way of life and culture'

Peter MacLeod
STORNOWAY GAZETTE

Some other books published by **LUATH** PRESS

SOCIAL HISTORY

The Crofting Years

Francis Thompson
ISBN 0 946487 06 5 PBK £5.95

Crofting is much more than a way of life. It is a storehouse of cultural, linguistic and moral values which holds together a scattered and struggling rural population. This book fills a blank in the written history of crofting over the last two centuries. Bloody conflicts and gunboat diplomacy, treachery, compassion, music and story: all figure in this mine of information on crofting in the Highlands and Islands of Scotland.

'I would recommend this book to all who are interested in the past, but even more so to those who are interested in the future survival of our way of life and culture.'
STORNOWAY GAZETTE

'A cleverly planned book ... the story told in simple words which compel attention ... [by] a Gaelic speaking Lewisman with specialised knowledge of the crofting community.'
BOOKS IN SCOTLAND

'The book is a mine of information on many aspects of the past, among them the homes, the food, the music and the medicine of our crofting forebears.'
John M Macmillan, erstwhile CROFTERS COMMISSIONER FOR LEWIS AND HARRIS

'This fascinating book is recommended to anyone who has the interests of our language and culture at heart.'
Donnie Maclean, DIRECTOR OF AN COMUNN GAIDHEALACH, WESTERN ISLES

'Unlike many books on the subject, Crofting Years combines a radical political approach to Scottish crofting experience with a ruthless realism which while recognising the full tragedy and difficulty of his subject never descends to sentimentality or nostalgia.'
CHAPMAN

LUATH GUIDES TO SCOTLAND

'Gentlemen, We have just returned from a six week stay in Scotland. I am convinced that Tom Atkinson is the best guidebook author I have ever read, about any place, any time.'
Edward Taylor, LOS ANGELES

These guides are not your traditional where-to-stay and what-to-eat books. They are companions in the rucksack or car seat, providing the discerning traveller with a blend of fiery opinion and moving description. Here you will find *'that curious pastiche of myths and legend and history that the Scots use to describe their heritage ... what battle happened in which glen between which clans; where the Picts sacrificed bulls as recently as the 17th century ... A lively counterpoint to the more standard, detached guidebook ... Intriguing.'*
THE WASHINGTON POST

These are perfect guides for the discerning visitor or resident to keep close by for reading again and again, written by authors who invite you to share their intimate knowledge and love of the areas covered.

South West Scotland

Tom Atkinson
ISBN 0 946487 04 9 PBK £4.95

This descriptive guide to the magical country of Robert Burns covers Kyle, Carrick, Galloway, Dumfries-shire, Kirkcudbrightshire and Wigtownshire. Hills, unknown moors and unspoiled beaches grace a land steeped in history and legend and portrayed with affection and deep delight.

An essential book for the visitor who yearns to feel at home in this land of peace and grandeur.

LUATH PRESS LIMITED

The Lonely Lands
Tom Atkinson
ISBN 0 946487 10 3 PBK £4.95

A guide to Inveraray, Glencoe, Loch Awe, Loch Lomond, Cowal, the Kyles of Bute and all of central Argyll written with insight, sympathy and loving detail. Once Atkinson has taken you there, these lands can never feel lonely. 'I have sought to make the complex simple, the beautiful accessible and the strange familiar,' he writes, and indeed he brings to the land a knowledge and affection only accessible to someone with intimate knowledge of the area.

A must for travellers and natives who want to delve beneath the surface.

'Highly personal and somewhat quirky... steeped in the lore of Scotland.'
THE WASHINGTON POST

The Empty Lands
Tom Atkinson
ISBN 0 946487 13 8 PBK £4.95

The Highlands of Scotland from Ullapool to Bettyhill and Bonar Bridge to John O'Groats are landscapes of myth and legend, 'empty of people, but of nothing else that brings delight to any tired soul,' writes Atkinson. This highly personal guide describes Highland history and landscape with love, compassion and above all sheer magic.

Essential reading for anyone who has dreamed of the Highlands.

Roads to the Isles
Tom Atkinson
ISBN 0 946487 01 4 PBK £4.95

Ardnamurchan, Morvern, Morar, Moidart and the west coast to Ullapool are included in this guide to the Far West and Far North of Scotland. An unspoiled land of mountains, lochs and silver sands is brought to the walker's toe-tips (and to the reader's fingertips) in this stark, serene and evocative account of town, country and legend.

For any visitor to this Highland wonderland, Queen Victoria's favourite place on earth.

Highways and Byways in Mull and Iona
Peter Macnab
ISBN 0 946487 16 2 PBK £4.25

'The Isle of Mull is of Isles the fairest, Of ocean's gems 'tis the first and rarest.' So a local poet described it a hundred years ago, and this recently revised guide to Mull and sacred Iona, the most accessible islands of the Inner Hebrides, takes the reader on a delightful tour of these rare ocean gems, travelling with a native whose unparalleled knowledge and deep feeling for the area unlock the byways of the islands in all their natural beauty.

The Speyside Holiday Guide
Ernest Cross
ISBN 0 946487 27 8 PBK £4.95

Toothache in Tomintoul? Golf in Garmouth? Whatever your questions, Ernest Cross has the answers in this witty and knowledgeable guide to Speyside, one of Scotland's most popular holiday centres. A must for visitors and residents alike – there are still secrets to be discovered here!

NATURAL SCOTLAND
Rum: Nature's Island
Magnus Magnusson KBE
ISBN 0 946487 32 4 PBK £7.95

Rum: Nature's Island is the fascinating story of a Hebridean island from the earliest times through to the Clearances and its period as the sporting playground of a Lancashire industrial magnate, and on to its rebirth as a National Nature Reserve, a model for the active ecological management of Scotland's wild places.

Thoroughly researched and written in a lively accessible style, the book includes comprehensive coverage of the island's geology, animals and plants, and people, with a special chapter on the Edwardian extravaganza of Kinloch Castle. There is practical information for visitors to what was once known as 'the Forbidden Isle';

the book provides details of bothy and other accommodation, walks and nature trails. It closes with a positive vision for the island's future: biologically diverse, economically dynamic and ecologically sustainable.

Rum: Nature's Island is published in co-operation with Scottish Natural Heritage (of which Magnus Magnusson is Chairman) to mark the 40th anniversary of the acquistion of Rum by its predecessor, the Nature Conservancy.

WALK WITH LUATH

Mountain Days & Bothy Nights
Dave Brown and Ian Mitchell
ISBN 0 946487 15 4 PBK £7.50
Acknowledged as a classic of mountain writing still in demand ten years after its first publication, this book takes you into the bothies, howffs and dosses on the Scottish hills. Fishgut Mac, Desperate Dan and Stumpy the Big Yin stalk hill and public house, evading gamekeepers and Royalty with a camaraderie which was the trademark of Scots hillwalking in the early days.

'*The fun element comes through ... how innocent the social polemic seems in our nastier world of today ... the book for the rucksack this year.*'
Hamish Brown, SCOTTISH MOUNTAINEERING CLUB JOURNAL

'*The doings, sayings, incongruities and idiosyncrasies of the denizens of the bothy underworld ... described in an easy philosophical style ... an authentic word picture of this part of the climbing scene in latter-day Scotland, which, like any good picture, will increase in charm over the years.*'
Iain Smart, SCOTTISH MOUNTAINEERING CLUB JOURNAL

'*The ideal book for nostalgic hillwalkers of the 60s, even just the armchair and public house variety ... humorous, entertaining, informative, written by*

two men with obvious expertise, knowledge and love of their subject.'
SCOTS INDEPENDENT

'*Fifty years have made no difference. Your crowd is the one I used to know ... [This] must be the only complete dossers' guide ever put together.*'
Alistair Borthwick, author of the immortal *Always a Little Further.*

The Joy of Hillwalking
Ralph Storer
ISBN 0 946487 28 6 PBK £6.95
Apart, perhaps, from the joy of sex, the joy of hillwalking brings more pleasure to more people than any other form of human activity.

'*Alps, America, Scandinavia, you name it – Storer's been there, so why the hell shouldn't he bring all these various and varied places into his observations ... [He] even admits to losing his virginity after a day on the Aggy Ridge ... Well worth its place alongside Storer's earlier works.*'
TAC

LUATH WALKING GUIDES
The highly respected and continually updated guides to the Cairngorms.

'*Particularly good on local wildlife and how to see it*'
THE COUNTRYMAN

Walks in the Cairngorms
Ernest Cross
ISBN 0 946487 09 X PBK £3.95
This selection of walks celebrates the rare birds, animals, plants and geological wonders of a region often believed difficult to penetrate on foot. Nothing is difficult with this guide in your pocket, as Cross gives a choice for every walker, and includes valuable tips on mountain safety and weather advice.
Ideal for walkers of all ages and skiers waiting for snowier skies.

LUATH PRESS LIMITED

Short Walks in the Cairngorms
Ernest Cross
ISBN 0 946487 23 5 PBK £3.95
Cross wrote this volume after overhearing a walker remark that there were no short walks for lazy ramblers in the Cairngorm region. Here is the answer: rambles through scenic woods with a welcoming pub at the end, birdwatching hints, glacier holes, or for the fit and ambitious, scrambles up hills to admire vistas of glorious scenery. Wildlife in the Cairngorms is unequalled elsewhere in Britain, and here it is brought to the binoculars of any walker who treads quietly and with respect.

BIOGRAPHY

On the Trail of Robert Service
Wallace Lockhart
ISBN 0 946487 24 3 PBK £5.95
Known worldwide for his verses 'The Shooting of Dan McGrew' and 'The Cremation of Sam McGee', Service has woven his spell for Boy Scouts and learned professors alike. He chronicled the story of the Klondike Gold Rush, wandered the United States and Canada, Tahiti and Russia to become the bigger-than-life Bard of the Yukon. Whether you love or hate him, you can't ignore this cult figure. The book is a must for those who haven't yet met Robert Service.

'The story of a man who claimed that he wrote verse for those who wouldn't be seen dead reading poetry ... this enthralling biography will delight Service lovers in both the Old World and the New.'
SCOTS INDEPENDENT

Come Dungeons Dark
John Taylor Caldwell
ISBN 0 946487 19 7 PBK £6.95
Glasgow anarchist Guy Aldred died with 10p in his pocket in 1963 claiming there was better company in Barlinnie Prison than in the Corridors of Power. 'The Red Scourge' is remembered here by one who worked with him and spent 27 years as part of his turbulent household, sparring with Lenin, Sylvia Pankhurst and others as he struggled for freedom for his beloved fellow-man.

'The welcome and long-awaited biography of ... one of this country's most prolific radical propagandists ... Crank or visionary? ... whatever the verdict, the Glasgow anarchist has finally been given a fitting memorial.'
THE SCOTSMAN

Bare Feet and Tackety Boots
Archie Cameron
ISBN 0 946487 17 0 PBK £7.95
The island of Rhum before the First World War was the playground of its rich absentee landowner. A survivor of life a century gone tells his story. Factors and schoolmasters, midges and poaching, deer, ducks and MacBrayne's steamers: here social history and personal anecdote create a record of a way of life gone not long ago but already almost forgotten. This is the story the gentry couldn't tell.

'This book is an important piece of social history, for it gives an insight into how the other half lived in an era the likes of which will never be seen again.'
FORTHRIGHT MAGAZINE

'The authentic breath of the pawky, country-wise estate employee.'
THE OBSERVER

'Well observed and detailed account of island life in the early years of this century'
THE SCOTS MAGAZINE

'A very good read with the capacity to make the reader chuckle. A very talented writer.'
STORNOWAY GAZETTE

LUATH PRESS LIMITED

Seven Steps in the Dark
Bob Smith
ISBN 0 946487 21 9 PBK £8.95

'The story of his 45 years working at the faces of seven of Scotland's mines ... full of dignity and humanity ... unrivalled comradeship ... a vivid picture of mining life with all its heartbreaks and laughs.'
SCOTTISH MINER

Bob Smith went into the pit when he was fourteen years old to work with his father. They toiled in a low seam, just a few inches high, lying in the coal dust and mud, getting the coal out with pick and shovel. This is his story, but it is also the story of the last forty years of Scottish coalmining. A staunch Trades Unionist, one of those once described as "the enemy within", his life shows that in fact he has been dedicated utterly to the betterment of his fellow human beings.

HUMOUR/HISTORY
Revolting Scotland
Jeff Fallow
ISBN 0 946487 23 1 PBK £5.95
No Heiland Flings, tartan tams and kilty dolls in this witty and cutting cartoon history of bonnie Scotland frae the Ice Age tae Maggie Thatcher.

'An ideal gift for all Scottish teenagers.'
SCOTS INDEPENDENT

'The quality of the drawing [is] surely inspired by Japanese cartoonist Keiji Nakazawa whose books powerfully encapsulated the horror of Hiroshima ... refreshing to see a strong new medium like this.'
CHAPMAN

MUSIC AND DANCE
Highland Balls and Village Halls
Wallace Lockhart
ISBN 0 946487 12 X PBK £6.95

'Acknowledged as a classic in Scottish dancing circles throughout the world. Anecdotes, Scottish history, dress and dance steps are all included in this 'delightful little book, full of interest ... both a personal account and an understanding look at the making of traditions.'
NEW ZEALAND SCOTTISH COUNTRY DANCES MAGAZINE

'A delightful survey of Scottish dancing and custom. Informative, concise and opinionated, it guides the reader across the history and geography of country dance and ends by detailing the 12 dances every Scot should know – the most famous being the Eightsome Reel, "the greatest longest, rowdiest, most diabolically executed of all the Scottish country dances".'
THE HERALD

'A pot-pourri of every facet of Scottish country dancing. It will bring back memories of petronella turns and poussettes and make you eager to take part in a Broun's reel or a dashing white sergeant!'
DUNDEE COURIER AND ADVERTISER

'An excellent an very readable insight into the traditions and customs of Scottish country dancing. The author takes us on a tour from his own early days jigging in the village hall to the characters and traditions that have made our own brand of dance popular throughout the world.'
SUNDAY POST

POETRY

The Jolly Beggars or 'Love and Liberty'

Robert Burns

ISBN 0 946487 02 2 HB 8.00

Forgotten by the Bard himself, the redis-covery of this manuscript caused storms of acclaim at the turn of the 19th centu-ry. Yet it is hardly known today. It was set to music to form the only cantata ever written by Burns. SIR WALTER SCOTT wrote: 'Laid in the very lowest department of low life, the actors being a set of strolling vagrants ... extravagant glee and outrageous frolic ... not, per-haps, to be paralleled in the English lan-guage.' This edition is printed in Burns' own handwriting with an informative introduction by Tom Atkinson.

'The combination of facsimile, lively John Hampson graphics and provocative com-ment on the text makes for enjoyable reading.'
THE SCOTSMAN

Poems to be Read Aloud

selected and introduced by Tom Atkinson

ISBN 0 946487 00 6 PBK £3.00

This personal collection of doggerel and verse ranging from the tear-jerking 'Green Eye of the Yellow God' to the rarely-printed bawdy 'Eskimo Nell' has a lively cult following. Much borrowed and rarely returned, this is a book for reading aloud in very good company, preferably after a dram or twa. You are guaranteed a warm welcome if you arrive at a gathering with this little vol-ume in your pocket.

'The essence is the audience.'
Tom Atkinson

Luath Press Limited

committed to publishing well written books worth reading

LUATH PRESS takes its name from Robert Burns, whose little collie Luath (*Gael.*, swift or nimble) tripped up Jean Armour at a wedding and gave him the chance to speak to the woman who was to be his wife and the abiding love of his life. Burns called one of *The Twa Dogs* Luath after Cuchullin's hunting dog in Ossian's *Fingal*. Luath Press grew up in the heart of Burns country, and now resides a few steps up the road from Burns' first lodgings in Edinburgh's Royal Mile.

Luath offers you distinctive writing with a hint of unexpected pleasures.

Most UK bookshops either carry our books in stock or can order them for you. To order direct from us, please send a £sterling cheque, postal order, international money order or your credit card details (number, address of cardholder and expiry date) to us at the address below. Please add post and packing as follows: UK – £1.00 per delivery address; overseas surface mail – £2.50 per delivery address; overseas airmail – £3.50 for the first book to each delivery address, plus £1.00 for each additional book by airmail to the same address. If your order is a gift, we will happily enclose your card or message at no extra charge.

Luath Press Limited
543/2 Castlehill
The Royal Mile
Edinburgh EH1 2ND

Telephone: 0131 225 4326
Fax: 0131 225 4324
email: gavin.macdougall@luath.co.uk
Website: www.luath.co.uk